Planning
Church
Events
With Ease

How to Make It Happen

Planning Church Events With Ease

V. KERRY INMAN

Ministry Resources Library

Zondervan Publishing House • Grand Rapids, MI

PLANNING CHURCH EVENTS WITH EASE
Copyright © 1988 by V. Kerry Inman

MINISTRY RESOURCES LIBRARY is an imprint of Zondervan Publishing House, 1415 Lake Drive S.E., Grand Rapids, Michigan, 49506.

Library of Congress Cataloging in Publication Data

Inman, V. Kerry
    Planning church events with ease.

    1. Church management. 2. Christian leadership. I. Title.
BV652.I56   1988   254'.6   87-31523
ISBN 0-310-40461-4

Edited by Joseph Comanda
Designed by Louise Bauer
Illustrated by Joe Van Severen

Printed in the United States of America

88   89   90   91   92   93 / CH / 10   9   8   7   6   5   4   3   2   1

To Byron C. Cassel

Retired vice-president of the Reading Railroad
and in retirement the business manager of
Pinebrook Junior College.

Through hard work and diligence,
he made things happen.

CONTENTS

Charts and Diagrams   9
Acknowledgments   10
Preface   11
Introduction: How This Book Works   15

PLANNING PHASE

1. "Your Mission, Should You Decide to Accept
   It . . ."   21
   Stage 1: Receiving the mission
2. "What in the World Are We Doing *This* For?"   25
   Stage 2: Establishing the purpose, goals, and objectives
3. Exploring Your Options   37
   Stage 3: Exploring courses of action
   Stage 4: Preparing estimates
4. The Big Decision   49
   Stage 5: Selecting a course of action

PREPARATION PHASE

5. Organizing for Action   61
   Stage 1: Identifying necessary tasks
   Stage 2: Scheduling preparatory tasks
6. Getting Down to Work   71
   Stage 3: Taking pre-event actions
7. "If Anything Can Go Wrong, It Will"   76
   Stage 4: Planning for contingencies

OUT OF PHASE

8. Good Leaders   91
9. Good Followers   96
10. Good Organization   102
11. More on Decision Making   112

CONDUCT PHASE

12. The Event at Last   119
     Stage 1: Executing the plan
     Stage 2: Supervising the event
     Stage 3: Executing contingencies
     Stage 4: Taking post-event actions
Epilogue   126
Appendix   128

CHARTS AND DIAGRAMS

The Inman Model for making it happen   17, 129
Purpose, goals, and objectives   31, 131
Possibilities   41
Manpower requirements   46–47
Sequence-of-tasks calendar: women's retreat   67
Sequence-of-tasks calendar: Boy Scout outing   68, 138
Sequence of component tasks: primary task #3   69
Contingency plans: East Moose Falls Community Church
    Sunday school picnic   80, 139–40
Battalion staff structure   103
Event staff structure   104
Simple event staff structure   105
Broad organization structure   107
Tall organization structure   108
Lopsided organization structure   109
Snarled organization structure   110

ACKNOWLEDGMENTS

If you are an experienced planner you may already be familiar with many of the techniques in this book. You may even consider some of them to be your innovations. If so, I apologize in advance for not recognizing the source. I have relied largely on my own experiences for my ideas. If I have borrowed from any written source in particular, I would have to say it was *Fleet Marine Force Manual 3–1, Command and Staff Action*. It is available from the U.S. Government Printing Office.

I would also like to express my appreciation to Dan Farrell, Phil Veitch, and Ken Richards, who read the manuscript and offered helpful comments.

PREFACE

What does a Sunday school picnic have in common with a battalion of marines landing on a hostile beach? More than you might think. Both require extensive advance planning and preparation—not to mention close coordination on the day of the event.

"True," you may say, "but hardly worth mentioning." If you had been at Gallipoli—the classic example of a poorly planned beach landing—or some of the Sunday school picnics I've been at, maybe—just maybe—you would understand why I mention it.

Planning, preparation, coordination: these things matter. Maybe you think you could manage a Sunday school picnic without too much trouble. But what about a conference or a workshop or a campaign? Every church could use some help in planning its programs.

As church leaders we tend not to think very much about what it takes to make something happen, but the marines have thought about it, so why not learn from them? After all, if they can bring off something as complicated as an amphibious landing, surely they can teach us something.

This idea first came to me a few years ago after returning from summer reserve duty as an infantry battalion executive officer with the U. S. Marine Corps. I thought to myself, "If the marines can pull off something like Iwo Jima, why do I always wind up at the Sunday school picnic with ice cream and no spoons? Someone needs to write a book about how to make things happen."

So that's what I did.

Do you realize that if a battalion of a thousand marines were landing on a hostile beach tomorrow, I as the executive officer could find out not just which landing vehicle any one of those thousand men was going ashore in, but exactly how much ammunition, food, and water he would be carrying, the ship he would be debarking, the time he would be debarking, and the time he would be landing on the beach? If I were really interested, I could find out where in any particular landing vehicle any particular man would be sitting. The marine amphibious assaults of the Second World War were perhaps among the most carefully planned military events in history, and we owe our freedom in part to this fact. Indeed, there are many ex-marines living today who can thank the planners for their lives.

"Hey, Major!" you say. "Quit running on about the marines and make it happen!"

All right then, let's get on with it!

Planning
Church
Events
With Ease

INTRODUCTION:
HOW THIS BOOK WORKS

Suppose someone asks you to plan a church event such as the annual church supper. You say yes without thinking. After all, you were brought up to be a willing worker. Moments later it hits you, but by then it's too late. You wonder, "How am I ever going to do it?"

Well, you could start by reading this book. It's all about how to make events happen—events as simple as church suppers and Sunday school picnics or as complex as workshops and conferences—and it's written especially with churches and other nonprofit organizations in mind.

It's amazing how little has been written on the subject of planning events. There's a lot of literature on planning in general—financial planning, long-range planning, even family planning. But little has been written that helps laypeople to plan an event. Perhaps it's because events can be so different, and thus each event seems to require a totally different planning strategy. If you can't see the continuity in planning events, how can you write about it?

In my preface I suggested similarities between a Sunday school picnic and a beach landing. Clearly, the events themselves are quite different, but odd as it may seem, there really is a marked continuity in the way the marines plan an amphibious operation and the way a church plans a Sunday school picnic. The similarities occur in what they do to make *it* —the event—happen.

THE INMAN MODEL

In this book I will be developing a model for making an event happen that I call "the Inman Model." (Why not, everybody else names things after themselves!) It's a model drawn from the way military operations are planned, but I've generalized it for any event. Basically that means I left out information like "fire support planning" and "casualty estimating"—things we shouldn't need at church suppers—and I "civilianized" (a truly military term) the jargon.

The model has three main parts:

```
┌─────────────────────────────┐
│  PLANNING PHASE             │
└─────────────────────────────┘
     ┌─────────────────────────────┐
     │  PREPARATION PHASE          │
     └─────────────────────────────┘
          ┌─────────────────────────────┐
          │  CONDUCT PHASE              │
          └─────────────────────────────┘
```

Almost anything you make happen in life involves these three phases whether you think of it that way or not. If you're conscious of them as phases, you're more likely to do a good job of whatever it is you want to make happen.

The *planning phase* comes first. That's when you make the decision about what should happen. Suppose you're asked to plan a family get-together. You have to think about a number of things. First of all, is it a good idea? What's the purpose of it? Which cousins should you include? What kinds of activities will you have? Where will you hold it? When should you have it? You could just "wing it" and deal with issues as they arise, but you're better off thinking through answers to these questions right at the start. That's what the planning phase is for.

After the planning phase is completed, the *preparation phase* begins. It's when you begin taking steps toward making the planned event a reality. You ask family members to come and suggest what each one should bring. You make reservations. You arrange for someone to get the invalid aunt out of the

THE INMAN MODEL FOR MAKING IT HAPPEN

PLANNING PHASE

1. Receiving the mission

2. Establishing the purpose, goals, and objectives

3. Exploring courses of action

4. Preparing estimates

5. Selecting a course of action

PREPARATION PHASE

1. Identifying necessary tasks

2. Scheduling preparatory tasks

3. Taking pre-event actions

4. Planning for contingencies

CONDUCT PHASE

1. Executing the plan

2. Supervising the event

3. Executing contingencies

4. Taking post-event actions

nursing home. In short, you see to it that everything is in place for the day of the event.

The *conduct phase* begins on "D day," the day of the event. The time for planning is over. You've made all the preparations. Now you're ready to begin. You pack the car and drive to the park. You unload the car. You start the charcoal grill. It begins to rain! You activate your contingency plan and invite everyone to your house. You spend three days cleaning up. All these activities are part of the conduct phase.

Of course, reality is never as simple as any model, and the work of making an event happen doesn't always divide neatly into three distinct phases. You may be changing the plans right down to the day of the event, and you may start with some of the preparations before the planning is over. Even so, the idea of phases is a valid one, and each phase is named for its predominant activity.

The rest of this book takes you through the steps of making an event happen using this model. We'll go over the model in great detail and look at each of the stages in each phase. Sometimes a chapter will cover more than one stage. Whenever a new stage starts, you'll be told the phase it belongs to, the name of the stage, and a list of things to write down in that stage. I've also included chapters on leaders, followers, and principles of organization. Finally, the appendix provides a quick-reference guide to the stages of the model.

There are some things I left out of this book. Pious readers will look in vain for mention of prayer or the Holy Spirit. I believe that little can be accomplished without prayer and the guidance of the Holy Spirit. Yet the issue of how they relate to planning is a complex one. It seemed better left to another, more theological book.

PLANNING PHASE

1

"YOUR MISSION, SHOULD YOU DECIDE TO ACCEPT IT ..."

PLANNING PHASE

1. Receiving the mission

What to write down: A description of the mission.

The whole process of making something happen begins with somebody asking you to do it. At that point, we could say that you had received a mission. Here's how it might happen for a Sunday school picnic.

The board of the East Moose Falls Community Church in East Moose Falls, Maine, is in session. Someone says, "We ought to have a Sunday school picnic again this year!" After some inconclusive discussion as to where and when, someone else suggests appointing a committee to organize it. Then there's more discussion about who should head it, and Mark Fischer's name comes up. No other names get mentioned, and everyone is looking at Mark expectantly. The pastor says, "What do you think, Mark?" Mark says he'll do it if there's a motion to that effect. The motion is made and seconded. All are in favor. For better or worse, Mark has just received a mission: to plan and conduct a Sunday school picnic.

About the same time that the board asks Mark to organize the Sunday school picnic, the governing board of the American

Association of Conference Managers (AACM) has a meeting. The board resolves that a subcommittee should be appointed to plan and conduct a conference on effective conference planning. The subcommittee meets and appoints Julie Daniels as conference manager. Her responsibilities will be different from Mark's in magnitude, but you may be surprised to find how closely her methodology will resemble his.

PROBLEMS OF AMBIGUITY

Mark is ready to move ahead on the Sunday school picnic, so he calls the committee together for its first meeting. Since it involves the Sunday school, he invites Jerry Perkins, the Sunday school superintendent. Jerry has news for Mark. It turns out that the education committee has already planned a picnic for the Sunday school. Nobody ever told Mark about it, of course, but Jerry just assumed he and his committee would do it. They always have.

Clearly Mark and Jerry have a problem of ambiguity. It's not clear who's in charge. And they're going to have to do something about it. They're going to have to go back to the church board and get the issue of who is responsible for the picnic clarified.

The act of receiving a mission may not seem to require any effort on your part. After all, someone else is giving you something to do. Actually it does. It's your job to make sure that the scope of your mission and the extent of your authority are clear before you take up your mission. If such issues remain ambiguous they can lead to later misunderstandings and confusion, and they may even jeopardize the whole event. You're better off resolving them at the start.

And what about the scope of your mission? What exactly *have* you been asked to do? That should be spelled out quite clearly. Our friend Julie was asked to plan a conference on conferences. Is it supposed to be a conference to train conference managers or a conference for people who are already conference managers? And what is a conference manager? Are we talking professionals here or amateurs?

Then there is the matter of authority. When you receive a

mission it might not be clear what authority you have been given, if any. Do you have the authority to make all the decisions? Remember, this usually includes the authority to have people angry with you if they don't like your decisions! Again, for Julie this is a fairly serious issue. She needs to know how much she can do on her own. Is she permitted to make financial obligations on behalf of the organization? Can she, for example, place a deposit on the hotel reservations? Can she contract with a caterer?

When an entire committee or board receives a mission, matters can get even more complicated. In a later chapter we will discuss more thoroughly the subject of boards and committees planning and executing events, but we need just a few words here about committees receiving a mission. When a committee is appointed to plan and execute an event, the question of who the committee is needs to be answered. It sounds dumb I know, but sometimes the instructions are vague as to who appointed the committee, who is on the committee, who is chairing it, and when the committee will meet. Enthusiastic committee members may grow frustrated if their mission seems nebulous. Things go a lot more smoothly if these basic issues of mission are resolved at the start.

RESOLVING AMBIGUITIES

The only way to resolve ambiguities is to go back to the organization that gave you the job and ask for clarification. If you're not careful, however, your answers may not be any clearer than your original instructions and could just lend more confusion.

A good approach is to write a resolution or job description and go back and ask, "Is this want you want me to do?" If the answer is yes, then you have clarified the matter. You must be careful here to ascertain that the governing board or authority really understands and supports what you've written. If they only "rubber stamp" it, and later they don't like what you've done, they may accuse you of writing your own job description. Make sure that your board supports in principle and spirit any authority you ask to be given.

IMPLIED MISSION

Sometimes you don't receive an explicit mission assignment for an event. Instead it comes from tradition or the position you hold. I suppose that's what happened with Jerry and the education committee. Nobody asked him and his committee to organize the picnic, and it probably doesn't say in any job description that he has the authority to call one. He probably doesn't even *have* a job description. But for as far back as anyone can remember Sunday school superintendents have always planned and run the Sunday school picnics, so there is certainly clear precedent for what he did. In effect, he received his mission to conduct the Sunday school picnic when he was appointed to the position.

Of course the problem with implied missions is that they can lead to misunderstandings unless they are spelled out. If Jerry had checked with the board before making his plans, he could have avoided confusion.

By the way, Mark's fellow board members were very apologetic about the mix-up. They considered themselves to blame. They should have known how things had been done in previous years, but boards have short memories. Anyway, the board made two decisions. First, since Jerry and his committee have already done the planning this year, they should stay in charge. Second, since the education committee has enough responsibilities planning the church's education programs, a special committee should handle the picnic in the future. Let's hope somebody remembers next year.

However you receive your mission, make sure you know what it is you've been asked to do and what authority you have to do it.

2

"WHAT IN THE WORLD ARE WE DOING *THIS* FOR?"

```
┌─────────────────────────────┐
│  PLANNING PHASE             │
└─────────────────────────────┘
      ┌─────────────────────────────────────┐
      │  2. Establishing the purpose, goals, and │
      │     objectives                          │
      └─────────────────────────────────────┘
```

What to write down: A statement of purpose.
A list of goals
A list of objectives

STARTING OUT WITH A PURPOSE

Another year has gone by, and Mark Fischer's fellow board members have once again given him an assignment. "We'd like you to head up a committee to plan and conduct the Sunday school picnic this year," they said. He asked if anyone had checked with Jerry. Apparently they had, so he agreed to do it. He made sure he understood exactly what they had in mind, and now he's ready to make his plans.

He calls the first meeting of the planning committee, and they start throwing around ideas about where to have it. Those who went to last year's picnic remember with some amusement how it ended dramatically with a surprise downpour. Someone comments on how poorly attended it was. Mark suggests it may have had to do with how far away it was. Certainly it couldn't have been the rain, for nobody was expecting that.

Someone else wonders whether people are all that interested in Sunday school picnics anymore. What *is* the purpose of a Sunday school picnic anyway?

That's a good question, and it's the first one they should ask—before they start talking about places to have it or anything else.

WHY ARE WE DOING THIS?

Any successful event must have a purpose—recognized or not. Setting the purpose clearly before you at the beginning keeps you from engaging in a useless exertion of time, energy, and money.

Have you ever asked, "Why are we doing this?" when you were in the middle of something with no way out? Then you should appreciate the value of defining the purpose beforehand. Sometimes it seems silly to define the purpose of an event, especially an annual event with a long tradition behind it. Yet those are the events most likely to elicit the question: "Why are we doing this?" Maybe if the planners asked the question beforehand, they'd discover that there really is no good answer.

Do you know what a "highway fire drill" is? Teenagers will stop their car in the middle of a road, jump out, run around it twice in opposite directions, jump back in, and take off. I have been to conferences that seemed as purposeless as that. The only difference was that the teenagers were having fun. Time, energy, and money are all valuable, so why waste them on pointless activities?

We're not just talking about a good reason for having the event. We can also refer to our stated purpose to see how well the various parts of the event relate to it. When we know what the purpose is, we find answers to questions like: Should we take an offering at the Sunday school picnic? Should we publish a list of participants in the week-long conference? It all depends on what the purpose is.

DEFINING THE EVENT

The first step in planning an event is to define what it is you're doing and why. You've been given a mission. Now it's up to you to work out the details that give the event its unique character. The best way to define the event is to state its purpose, goals, and objectives.

It may seem ludicrous to write up a twenty-page document articulating the purpose, goals, and objectives of a Sunday school picnic, but bear with me. That's not exactly what I'm suggesting. And remember, it was the Sunday school planning committee that brought up the question about purpose.

DETERMINING THE PURPOSE

The key word here is "determining." The purpose must be determined, not invented or created.

How do you go about determining an event's purpose? If the information you received when you were given the mission is rather scanty, try looking at the purpose of the sponsoring body. Virtually every event has a sponsoring body. The conference on conducting successful conferences is sponsored by the American Association of Conference Managers, and the Sunday school picnic, by the East Moose Falls Community Church. An event's purpose should be consistent with the stated purpose of its sponsoring organization.

The American Association of Conference Managers is a nonprofit corporation incorporated in the Commonwealth of Pennsylvania. The process of being granted nonprofit status required drawing up a statement of purpose that can now be found in the organization's bylaws and reads as follows:

THE PURPOSE OF THE ORGANIZATION shall be: to provide a professional organization for managers of conferences and to promote and conduct well planned and executed conferences in America.

Therefore, the purpose for the week-long conference in New York must—by law, no less—be subsidiary to this purpose.

With our East Moose Falls Sunday school picnic, the situation is not so simple. The church has always been there. There is no charter of corporation or bylaws. No one is even sure that there is a deed to the property. But the church does have a purpose—ask around.

27

It's to worship God, isn't it?

Well, this particular church is for the people of this community. I understand that back when the town was founded, Mr. Wittaker set aside this property for the town church.

If you ask me, even though you didn't, I'd say—of course you have to remember I was born in Scotland and didn't come here until I was eleven, and that of course has always made me a foreigner—I'd say it's the edification of the saints and the evangelization of the lost.

Every organization has a purpose however nebulously defined.

STATING THE PURPOSE

Not every event needs a written statement of purpose. Certainly our Sunday school picnic doesn't. Still, you should know what that purpose is and be able to articulate it clearly. The character of the event may differ radically if the purpose is stated differently. Is the purpose "to have fun (the edification of the saints)" or "to get some people saved (the evangelization of the lost)"? The successful planner has to have before him a clear statement of purpose.

What should a statement of purpose look like? It needs two characteristics. It should be simple; it should be broad.

It should be written in plain English (not legalese) and be as simple as you can make it. The purpose itself should also be simple—and as broad as possible. When you're thinking about purpose, you're trying to keep in mind the "big picture" of what the event is all about. Don't get bogged down in convoluted statements that loose sight of the forest for the trees.

Julie, the conference manager, drafted a statement of purpose for the conference on conferences. Let's look at it.

The purpose of the twenty-third annual conference on the conduct of conferences is to increase the awareness of conference managers regarding their own self worth as persons of professional standing as conference managers, and to promote meaningful dialogue between experienced conference managers and inexperienced persons and among each other, the conference will also attempt to increase the membership of the AACM by 10 percent and raise support for a lobbyist in Washington during the up and coming debate over House Bill 106 on the establishment of a federal agency to monitor conferences which is being established under the interstate commerce clause.

How would you say it rates as a statement of purpose? You certainly couldn't say it was simple. What would you say the purpose is? There appears to be more than one, doesn't there? In fact, if you pick your way carefully through all the clauses, you can find three: to bring conference managers together, to get new members, and to raise funds for lobbying. Would you say you were looking at the forest or the trees?

Clearly, the statement will need revision, but that's all right. The whole point of a first draft is to get something down on paper so you can work with it.

Julie needs to try again. This time she should keep in mind the two principles: simplicity and breadth. She should try to state in a few words a single purpose that will cover everything she hopes to accomplish. Here's the second draft.

The purpose of the twenty-third annual conference on the conduct of conferences is to promote professionalism among conference managers.

It's nice and tight this time, but shouldn't she say something about increasing membership and raising funds for lobbying? No, they're all part of increasing professionalism. They do need to be stated, but not in the statement of purpose. Julie can put them in the statement of goals and objectives for the event. Let's turn to that next.

GOALS AND OBJECTIVES

As with the statement of purpose, not every event needs a *written* statement of goals and objectives, but the successful planner needs to have them clearly in mind.

What exactly are goals and objectives, how are they different from each other, and how do they relate to the purpose?

Goals are general statements about the hoped–for results of the event. They amplify the purpose. *Objectives* are concrete statements about measurable results that can be used to determine if the goals were met.

The *goals* for the Sunday school picnic are probably as simple as this:

1. We want people to have fun.
2. We don't want anyone to get hurt.

The *objectives* may never be stated, but they're related to the goals:

1. People will laugh.
2. No one will go to the hospital.

Here the difference between goals and objectives is very clear. We do not actually see people having fun, we see them laughing. The objective is measurable or observable. The goal is general.

You might ask why we need both goals and objectives. Why not just have objectives? Because objectives and the statement of purpose, when both are stated properly, are remote from each other and need the goals as linking, amplifying information. All three statements—the purpose, goals, and objectives—are necessary to give a clear definition of the event. The relationship is illustrated in figure 2.1.

WRITING GOALS

It's probably easier to see the importance of both goals and objectives when we look at the goals and objectives of the conference on conferences. Again Julie, our planner, sat down and wrote a rough draft of the goals for the conference on conferences. Here's what she came up with:

Goals for the twenty-third annual conference on the conduct of conferences

1. To increase awareness of the need for professional conference planners and managers in our complex society
2. To provide for meaningful interaction between the members of the current organization

3. To increase the membership of the current organization
4. To establish the mechanism for fund raising necessary to obtain the services of a federal lobbyist

Notice that Julie used incomplete sentences when writing her goals and that they all start with an infinitive: "to increase," "to provide," "to establish."

Figure 2.1. **Purpose, Goals, and Objectives**

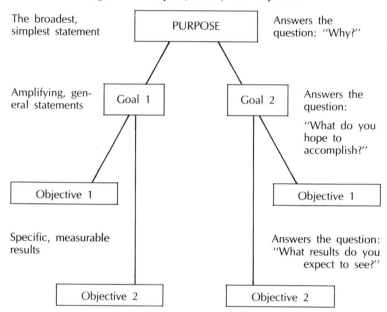

The statement of purpose is the starting point for everyone who will be involved with the conference planning and the execution of that plan. The goals go on to amplify the specific aspects of increased professionalism that it is believed the conference can obtain. Some people working on the conference planning staff will be concerned with only one goal, but they are all concerned with the same purpose. As conference manager, Julie has to plan a conference that will accomplish all these goals.

WRITING OBJECTIVES

Though she still had only a rough draft of her goals, Julie went ahead and wrote a draft of her objectives. From previous experience, she knew that writing the objectives would probably help point out potential problems with her goals. The draft of her objectives looked like this:

Objectives for the twenty-third annual conference on the conduct of conferences

Regarding Goal 1

a. To make sure that at least 10 percent of the attendees are not conference managers, but are executives of corporations or organizations which could make good use of a professional conference manager.

b. To have a workshop on the role of the professional conference manager in today's society.

Regarding Goal 2

a. To provide ???

Regarding Goal 3

a. To make sure that 20 percent of the attendees are nonmembers.

b. To sign up as new members 50 percent of the nonmembers attending the conference.

Regarding Goal 4

a. To obtain from members of the association a resolution regarding hiring a lobbyist.

b. To educate the members of the association regarding House Bill 106.

Notice that the objectives, like the goals, are stated in incomplete sentences starting with an infinitive. You can see also that each objective is linked to a specific goal and that there are sometimes several objectives for a given goal.

Unlike goals, objectives are supposed to be measurable. In fact, either during or after the conference, they should serve to indicate whether the goals were achieved. Objective 2 under Goal 3, for example, is clearly measurable. After the conference, Julie can add up the new members and determine if the objective was met. That, in turn, will tell her just how well they did at achieving their goal of increasing membership at the conference.

Objective 2 under Goal 4 is not measurable and will have to be revised, and she didn't write any objectives for Goal 2, but again this is a rough draft. Let them stand for now.

REFINING THE PURPOSE, GOALS, AND OBJECTIVES

Many people have trouble writing. They're so afraid of getting things wrong that they can't even get started. The secret is to jot ideas down without paying any attention to grammar, spelling, and punctuation. Later, after you've got your thoughts on paper, you can go back over them and refine them.

If you're not sure how to go about writing and revising, you can follow this general model, which is currently popular in college writing courses:

1. Get it down on paper.
2. Organize the thoughts, outlining the composition if necessary.

3. Rewrite (Steps 2 and 3 may have to be repeated more than once).

4. Proofread three times: once for clarity, once for grammar, and finally for spelling.

This process is perfectly suited to writing and revising goals and objectives. In fact, one approach you can use in your first draft is to write down goals in the order they occur to you, leaving plenty of room between them. If you think of objectives while you're still doing goals, jot them down under the appropriate goal.

When you're done with this first round, you can go back over everything, reorganizing goals or objectives into a more logical order if necessary, perhaps combining or splitting some or adding new ones. If you don't have to submit the results to any other group, you can stop the process when you're satisfied that you've got the goals and objectives you want. If you need a polished version for a submission, you can do the rewriting and proofreading necessary to get it into finished form.

Committees working together on goals and objectives can do the initial drafts using a blackboard or a large notepad on an easel and then let one of the members do the final proofreading and revisions.

Julie wasn't totally satisfied with her first version (pp. 30–31). She was aware of the problems we've already mentioned—especially the lack of any objectives for Goal 2. She started by reworking her goals. Her second try looked like this:

Goals for the twenty-third annual conference on the conduct of conferences

1. To increase awareness of the role professional conference managers can play in helping business and industry conduct conferences more efficiently and with greater success.

2. To provide for informal social interaction between the members of the current organization.

3. To increase the membership of the current organization.

4. To establish the mechanism for obtaining the services of and funding a federal lobbyist.

Most of the revisions involved only minor word changes, but the revision of Goal 2 illustrates why it is sometimes helpful to rough out objectives before revising the goals.

Julie hadn't been able to articulate an objective for Goal 2. Then she realized what the problem was. The goal was too vague. What's "meaningful interaction," anyway? What she realized she had in mind was the sort of thing that happens when people in the same business get together and develop friendships because of their mutual interests. As a goal this could best be stated as "providing the setting to encourage such interaction," but there is no way anyone can make friendships happen. She revised the goal so it was more realistic.

She then went on and revised her objectives as follows:

Objectives for the twenty-third annual conference on the conduct of conferences

Regarding Goal 1

1. To make sure that at least 10 percent of the attendees are not conference managers, but are executives of corporations or organizations that could use a professional manager.
2. To have workshops on how the professional conference manager can save firms money and get better results.
3. To provide a directory of professional conference managers to all conference attendees.

Regarding Goal 2

1. To provide at least three social functions of varying degrees of formality.
2. To provide coffee breaks and meals in a manner that will encourage informal conversation and group interaction.

Regarding Goal 3

1. To include among the conference attendees 20 percent nonmembers.
2. To sign up as new members 50 percent of the nonmembers attending the conference.

Regarding Goal 4

1. To conduct a workshop on House Bill 106 several times during the conference.

2. To get 100 percent of the membership to attend a session of the workshop on House Bill 106.

3. To obtain from members of the association a resolution regarding hiring a lobbyist.

GETTING ON WITH THE PLANNING

Do the purpose, goals, and objectives all have to be defined before moving on the the next step in the planning process? Not at all. In fact, it's actually a good idea to leave the objectives somewhat tentative until the next planning stage, but you should have the purpose established and be close to a final definition of goals.

Of course you can always revise. Too much revision defeats the purpose of defining a purpose and goals, but there's always room for improvement.

As Julie continued with her work, she realized that Objective 2 under Goal 2 was not measurable, and she revised it as follows:

2. To include daily morning and afternoon coffee breaks.

Then she added:

3. To provide a meal schedule that allows for leisurely dining.

Granted, you cannot remove the subjective element from objectives entirely, but the more measurable they are, the easier it is to evaluate how well you met them. When the conference is in full swing, Julie can go to the dining room of the hotel and see whether attendees have time to linger over their meals or whether they are being rushed through.

Thinking through the purpose, goals, and objectives for an event may seem like a pointless exercise, the kind of paperwork that only a bureaucrat could love. Properly done, however, it's actually a very valuable process that will bring into sharp focus for you what you're trying to accomplish and why.

3

EXPLORING YOUR OPTIONS

PLANNING PHASE

3. Exploring courses of action

What to write down: A list of alternatives.

Once Mark Fischer's committee had established the purpose, goals, and objectives, they were ready to think about where to have the picnic. After kicking it around awhile, they came up with three alternatives. They could go back to the shore again, have it at a state park, or use the Singer's back yard (Rachel Singer is on the committee and she offered the use of her yard and pool). They're all agreed that the various options will more or less accomplish the same goal. All they have to do is settle on one of them.

Julie Daniels is also exploring her options. She's committed to having the best possible conference. Now she needs to come up with some ideas on how to do that.

Both organizing groups are in the next planning stage. They're exploring courses of action. A course of action is simply a way of doing something, and the point of this stage is to come up with some good alternative courses of action that are consistent with the purpose of the event.

Eventually, they'll have to pick a single course of action,

the one that will best accomplish the stated purpose of their event, but they're not ready for that yet. They'll work up to it gradually.

First they need to come up with some alternatives, the more the merrier. Then they need to narrow down the possibilities to a few prime candidates. In the next stage, they'll examine those prime candidates more closely and estimate their cost. Only then will they be ready to select the best course of action.

COMING UP WITH ALTERNATIVES

Maybe the Sunday school picnic has been held at the seashore for as long as anyone can remember, and maybe the AACM has always had its annual conference at the same New York hotel. Why not just leave well enough alone, particularly if there haven't been any complaints?

That's certainly a valid approach. Remember, the point is to have the best possible event. If you're already doing it the best possible way, why change it?

Of course, that's not the usual case. Usually, there's plenty of room for improvement. Then too, circumstances may have changed. Maybe people are getting tired of going to the same place every year, or maybe the hotel is under new management and the rates have soared out of range. Or maybe this is a new event you've never done before, so there aren't any precedents for a course of action. Whatever the case, it's a good idea to consider alternatives.

At this point you should try to come up with as many fresh ideas as possible. Brainstorm. Make lists. Be innovative. Be traditional. Be both at once, if possible. Don't get bogged down yet in the details of implementing each alternative. That comes later. For now, just get those ideas out.

By the way, while we're on the subject of brainstorming, here's an important point to remember. One person can brainstorm, but if the event is being planned by a committee, it's important to get ideas from all the members. The best brainstorming sessions are those where everybody participates.

NARROWING THE POSSIBILITIES

Once you've generated as many ideas as you can, you're ready to get practical. Take a good, hard look at your list and try to pick out the most likely candidates. Three is a practical number. Pick out the three most likely distinct alternatives.

Now's the time to remember your purpose, goals, and objectives. You'll find, upon closer examination, that some courses of action that sounded brilliant at the time don't fit in so well with your purpose. Others will be impractical for other reasons.

The Sunday school picnic planning committee had it easy. They only had three courses of action, and they all seemed consistent with the stated purpose.

Things were more complicated for Julie. Neither the board nor the subcommittee had given any direction as to where, when, or how long the conference should be. She decided to get together with the subcommittee and have a brainstorming session. They came up with quite a few ideas.

Here's a sampling from their list.

Have it in New Orleans

Begin on a Friday night, end Sunday evening

A series of workshops

Begin with a formal ball

No long, drawn-out business meetings

Bob James should be the keynote speaker

San Francisco

New York

Atlantic City

When it came to narrowing down the possibilities, the committee noticed that many of the ideas were not mutually exclusive. Instead, they related to different aspects of the conference. Julie suggested breaking the list into categories. They ended up with a new list that resembled figure 3.1.

The committee now had four categories with a number of alternatives for each. Applying a little bit of statistics they discovered they had forty-eight possible courses of action

Figure 3.1. **Possibilities**

Location	Length	Character	Structure
New York	Weekend	Informal	Broad selection of activities
San Francisco	Full week	Formal	Uniform programs for all
New Orleans	Half-week and weekend		
Atlantic City			

(4x3x2x2). With six people on the subcommittee, that meant eight courses of action for each to prepare estimates on. This sounded like a lot of work! Since they were all professional conference planners, they decided to look at their stated purpose, goals, and objectives and pare down the possible courses of action for which estimates would be prepared. They settled on three:

1. A formal, week-long, varied conference in New York
2. An informal, weekend, uniform conference in San Francisco
3. An informal, half-week-plus-weekend, uniform conference in New Orleans

It is important to note that they didn't rule out any other possibilities at this point. They merely picked the three most likely possibilities for closer examination. Then they divided among them the work of preparing estimates.

PLANNING PHASE

4. Preparing estimates

What to write down: Formal estimates.

Once you've come up with some good alternative courses of action, you need to look at them more closely and estimate their cost. That will make it easier to decide on the best possible course of action.

An estimate need not be highly sophisticated. It all depends on the nature of the event. With the picnic, it's probably a matter of thinking through the answers to some questions. Who would come? How much work is involved? Is the park available? Can we afford it?

The answers to these questions come in the form of "if/then" statements. *If* it is at the shore, *then* it will have to be an all-day affair. *If* it's at the Singers', *then* it can be just an evening event. *If* it is in the evening, *then* it won't be very long. You've probably done this before, but you may not have thought of it as preparing estimates.

The conference on conferences is a more complex event with a considerably larger budget, so its estimating process should be more formal. Since it will probably involve cost comparisons of various hotels and convention halls, it should be written and detailed.

When the event is being planned by a committee, there are two ways to work on detailed estimates. One way is to have an estimate for each possible course of action prepared by a different person or subcommittee. The second way utilizes the special strengths of members or subcommittees. Members or subcommittees prepare estimates for those parts of each course of action related to their areas of expertise. For example, one subcommittee handles financial estimates, another looks at marketing.

Whether simple or complex, all estimates should address three basic considerations. I've called them benefits, work, and resources.

The first consideration is the benefits. How well does this course of action fulfill the purpose of the event? That covers a lot of questions. Will people attend? Will the people we want attend? Will they like it? Will they get anything out of it? Will they get the right things out of it?

The second consideration is the work. How difficult will it be to "pull it off"? Is there a lot of work involved? Does it require obtaining permits and making reservations? How large a staff will we need during the event?

The third consideration is the resources. Are the means to "pull it off" available? Do we have enough people to do the work? Do we have enough money? Is there a facility available?

Let's take a closer look at each of these aspects of making estimates.

IDENTIFYING THE BENEFITS

Identifying the benefits means to consider two basic questions. First, will the event accomplish its purpose and goals, and second, will the event appeal to people? The first question will have a more subjective answer than the second. You have to evaluate the purpose and goals of the proposed event and then state an opinion. It will be easy for anyone opposed to the course of action to dispute your opinion since it will be based largely on subjective judgment. Still, it's an important assessment to make and should be done with as much care as possible.

The second question may be less subjective, but determining the appeal of the event to people is by no means a science. It's more a matter of educated guesswork. Here are some of the basic considerations for determining the appeal:

1. How many will attend?
2. Who will attend: ages, sex, attitudes, and values of those attending?
3. What are their reasons for attending?
4. How satisfied will they be with this course of action?

You may want to ask other questions about other kinds of events. With a fund-raising event you might want to know whether you can attract those most willing and able to give. With an evangelistic meeting you'll want to know whether you're most likely to attract those who need to be evangelized or those already evangelized.

In making an estimate, you should stay away from comparisons between the different courses of action, and you should try not to let your own preferences for a particular course of action color your estimates. In other words, at this point you shouldn't be considering whether a picnic at the shore is better than one at the Singer's pool, only how many will be likely to attend one or the other.

IDENTIFYING THE WORK

Another important part of making an estimate is determining how much work is involved with a particular course of action. Here the chief problem is making sure your estimate is accurate. It's easy to underestimate by overlooking "incidental" tasks or by minimizing the amount of time it will require. Be sure to include *all* the work in your estimate, and make an effort to get realistic time estimates.

Now is a good time to introduce a distinction between tasks and actions. A task is a single job that needs to be done. An action is a particular way to accomplish the task. You need to get a charcoal grill. That's the task. You could borrow one from Charlie, who's on the committee. That's an action. It's one way the task can be accomplished. You could also borrow the grill from someone else, or you could buy or rent it. They're all actions which will accomplish the same task.

In preparing estimates you're dealing with tasks, not with particular actions to accomplish them. You should take account of the fact that you'll need to have meals at the conference, but you shouldn't get bogged down in the specific menu items. To use an example more related to work, your estimate may include a task like this: "We will need programs printed." But it shouldn't include a specific action like this: "We will need to find enough volunteers to put the programs together if we want to save money."

We also need to make another distinction between two different types of tasks: preparation tasks and conduct tasks. My definitions here are original so you won't be able to find them in a dictionary, but the concept is quite simple.

By preparation tasks I mean work that must be done before the event in preparation for it. In the case of the picnic that might include making reservations, locating a charcoal grill, and purchasing hot dogs.

Conduct tasks are jobs that must be done during or after the event. They would include things like starting the charcoal grill, cooking hot dogs, being a lifeguard, and supervising children's games, as well as cleaning up afterward and returning the grill.

The more complex the event, the more valuable this distinction becomes. Essentially, it provides a way of grouping tasks for more precise estimates. For one thing, some courses of action are heavier on conduct tasks while others are heavier on preparation tasks. By grouping tasks this way, it's easier to make valid comparisons. For another, the people doing the tasks will probably be different. With our conference on conferences, for example, the person who decides the menu for the banquet and contracts with the caterer will certainly not be involved in preparing the food.

For written estimates, start by simply listing the tasks that come to mind. Remember again the hints given in the previous chapter about writing goals and objectives—just get something down on paper first. Write all the tasks you can think about even if they're not systematically organized and may overlap. Then go back over the list combining and clarifying as necessary. If you have several pages, take a pair of scissors and cut and reorganize the tasks into groups. Make a couple of lists of the same tasks grouped differently. Make one list of similar tasks grouped together. Make another grouped according to related goals.

When you have finished these lists, organize them into a hierarchy of tasks. First, list the essential tasks *required* to execute the event broken down into conduct tasks and preparation tasks. Then make a separate list of additional tasks that aren't essential but might improve the quality of the event or its chances of success. You don't have to submit this supplementary list of nonessential tasks as part of the estimate, but you should have it on hand in case questions come up in later discussions.

Again bear in mind that the amount of work involved in planning needs to be proportional to the actual event. You probably don't need to bother making a written list of tasks for a small picnic, but you had better do it for a week-long conference.

IDENTIFYING THE RESOURCES

Finally the estimate must include a consideration of the resources necessary to accomplish the event. Most events require a combination of manpower, material, fiscal, and physical resources.

Manpower estimates answer questions about how many workers you need to bring off the event. How many volunteers need to bring food? How many drivers are needed? Will you need a master of ceremonies? Will you need a piano player? How big a cleanup crew do you need? These are the kinds of questions to ask? At this point don't worry about who will be the MC, just whether or not you will need one for that course of action. If you later decide on a different course of action, you may not need an MC.

To prepare a manpower estimate, go through the lists of tasks and add estimates of the number of workers you will need for each task. For a large undertaking involving paid workers or numerous volunteers, you may want to evaluate manpower in terms of full-time employees—one person working forty hours per week—and decimal equivalents of a full-time employee for part time and volunteer work. Julie's estimate for the conference on conferences looked like figure 3.3.

Figure 3.3. **Manpower Requirements**

1. For tasks that must be performed to execute the event
   a. Conduct tasks
      1) Day 1
         Manager: 1
         Secretary: 1
         Business manager: 1
         Program coordinator: 1
         Registration desk: 16
         Speakers' escorts: 10
         Problem solvers: 2
      2) Days 2–5
         Manager: 1
         Secretary: 1
         Business manager: 1
         Program coordinator: 1
         Registration desk: 2
         Speakers' escorts: 4

    Problem solvers: 2
  3) Day 6
    Manager: 1
    Secretary: 1
    Business manager: 1
    Program coordinator: 1
    Speakers' escorts: 4
    Problem solvers: 2
  4) Post-conference period for approximately 15 days
    Manager: .2
    Secretary: .5
    Business manager: 1
  b. Preparation tasks
    Manager: 1
    Secretary: .5
    Business manager: 1
    Program coordinator: 1
    Assistant program coordinators: 2

2. For nonessential tasks that will produce greater success
    Information booth: 4
    Lost-and-found: 2.5
    Entertainment coordinator: 1

Material estimates answer questions about materials and equipment. Do you need buses? Do you need a charcoal grill? How many hot dogs do you need? Do you need to bring chairs? Later when you have decided on the particular course of action to follow, you will deal with the issue of where and how to get the grill. A written material estimate can be a simple list of materials and equipment needed.

Fiscal estimates are even easier. You simply ask how much it will cost. With some larger events these estimates can include more complicated questions like "Will the people you want to attend this conference be willing to pay this much?" A written fiscal estimate is something you may already be very familiar with. It's called a budget.

You may also want to consider cash flow problems for larger events. For example, if people are going to pay in advance, will the money be there in time for you to pay your bills or do you need to take out a loan? A cash flow plan details income and expenses over segments of time and proposes financing as necessary. There is no standard format for a cash flow plan as there is for a budget.

Finally, *physical* estimates deal with the facilities. How much room do you need for breaks and for registration? How big an auditorium will you need? What about parking space? If a specific facility or location is being considered as the course of action, you will be asking questions like these: Is the park too far away? Is there room for a softball game and a volleyball game at the same time? Is there too much walking for some of the elderly to get from the parking lot to the beach?

Written physical estimates don't need to follow any standard format.

ESTIMATES OF PREPARATION AND CONDUCT

The distinction we made earlier between preparation tasks and conduct tasks run through all the resource estimates for larger events. In the case of manpower, for example, you want to know both how many people you'll need to prepare for the event and how many you'll need to get everything done on the day of the event. They showed up in our sample manpower estimates under preparation tasks and conduct tasks respectively. You should also make the same distinctions with material, fiscal, and physical estimates.

Finally, remember to include resource requirements for follow-up tasks after the event—things like cleaning up, paying bills, and returning equipment. Consider them additional conduct tasks.

When you've completed the estimates for all the alternative courses of action, you're finally in a position to make the big decision about what to do.

4

THE BIG DECISION

5. Selecting a course of action

What to write down: An outline of the plan for the event.

Sooner or later, if an operation is to be successful, planning must lead first to decisions and then to action. You have to decide what you want to happen and then get on with the preparations.

Selecting a course of action is not the only decision you will make in planning an event—but it's the primary one. With this decision the planning phase ends and the preparation phase begins.

But before we talk about the big decision, let's talk about how to make a good decision.

GOOD DECISIONS AND SOUND DECISIONS

Not all decisions are made the same way—not even all good decisions. Some very good decisions are the result of careful deliberation. Others are made on instinct. That leads us to an important distinction between good decisions and sound decisions.

A decision can only be called good in retrospect. After we see the results of a decision, we can judge whether or not it was a good one. A sound decision, on the other hand, is the best possible decision that can be made with the information available. Such a decision may later prove to be good or bad, but we will always look back at it as the best decision possible at the time given the knowledge we had then.

We all want to make good decisions, of course, but at the moment of decision the best we can do is make a sound decision. What's nice about sound decisions, though, is that they very often turn out to have been good decisions.

How then can we arrive at sound decisions? We have to review all the facts relating to the decision and make a judgment. No matter how many facts we review, and how long we think about it and study it, in the end somebody has to make a judgment. What we need is a model for making sure that all the factors weighing on the decision will be considered.

A MODEL FOR SOUND DECISIONS

Here is a general model for making sound decisions. Notice that its steps parallel in many ways the steps of the planning phase itself.

1. Define the issue
2. List the facts
3. Recognize the assumptions
4. Make estimates
5. Review goals and long-range plans
6. Analyze alternatives
7. Make the decision
8. Communicate the decision

AN EXAMPLE

To discuss decision making in general, we'll use an example unrelated to event planning. We'll watch how Sarah, a young woman deciding which of two colleges to attend, goes through the eight steps of the decision model.

1. *Define the issue*

Every decision involves an issue. It could be as simple as deciding yes or no, or it could involve a list of alternatives. Furthermore, the range of importance of the issues can be quite diverse, from Hamlet's anguished "to be or not to be" to a child's vacillation between chocolate and vanilla.

Whatever the issue, the first step is to make sure the issue is clear. What is it you are trying to make a decision about and what are the alternatives? It may all be perfectly evident, but often enough it isn't. I can recall several occasions on which people came to me for advice about a decision when the real problem was that they lacked a clear idea of what the issue was.

For Sarah, the alternatives are clear. She can either attend South Moose Falls State College or Innercity University. In some situations the alternatives may seem more complex, but the task here remains the same: to state alternatives clearly.

2. *List the facts*

The second step in arriving at a decision is to list the facts that have a bearing on the issue. The tuition at South Moose Falls State College is $2,500 per semester. At Innercity University it is $3,800. In addition, Sarah could live at home if she goes to South Moose Falls State College, but she would have to pay an additional $3,000 per semester for a room at Innercity University. All these are pertinent facts.

Other considerations that are really assumptions or opinions can sometimes get confused with facts. "Living in a dormitory will be fun," is not a fact. It is an opinion. "Adjusting to the life in the inner city will not be a major problem," is an assumption. At this stage of the game, we should follow the advice of Sergeant Friday: "Stick to the facts, Ma'am, only the facts."

3. *Recognize the assumptions*

In any decision-making process there are certain assumptions. This is neither good nor bad, only inevitable. Sometimes assumptions prove to be mistaken, but often they are the best guess at an outcome that can't be predicted with any certainty. The important thing is to recognize them for what they are.

Beyond that we can try to make assumptions as safe as possible by making sure we've checked whatever facts there might be to back them up. The conclusion that an assumption is not safe becomes a fact in itself.

Sarah found that she had made a couple of assumptions. She assumed that living at home would not inhibit her success in college and that adjusting to life in the inner city wouldn't be a major problem for her. Once she recognized them as assumptions, she did some checks to see how safe her assumptions were. After talking to friends who had commuted from home to college and had done well academically, she concluded that her first assumption was a safe one. She took a similar approach with her second assumption, but the results were less conclusive. She learned that some people had no problems at all, but that others never adjusted successfully. She decided in the end that it was not a safe assumption.

4. *Make estimates*

These must be distinguished from facts. Estimates are not certain and may include opinions and judgments, but they are, nevertheless, important considerations. Sarah estimated that she could earn about $2,000 on her summer vacation and that her parents could help her out with another $5,000. She concluded that she didn't have enough to go to the Innercity University unless she got a combination of scholarships or loans equaling $6,600 a year.

5. *Review goals and long-range plans*

Like so many of her fellow seniors, Sarah wasn't sure what she wanted to do with her life, but she realized that it had some bearing on her decision to go to college. For one thing, she wasn't sure whether she wanted to pursue a career or get married and have a family. The too, if she went for a career, she wasn't sure what it would be. She was good at art and had thought about becoming either a graphics artist or a fashion designer, but she didn't think she was ready to commit herself to either. She had learned that Innercity University only offered a degree in art history while South Moose Falls State College had separate majors in both graphics design and fashion design. Reviewing her goals—even though they were still fairly vague—led her to add these facts to her list.

6. *Analyze the alternatives*

Sarah tried to think through her alternatives to see what the outcome of each was likely to be. Going to Innercity University would be financially difficult (perhaps even impossible), but it would expose her to a new kind of life and give her a good foundation in the arts, and it was close to a lot of important galleries. Going to South Moose Falls State College would be cheaper (she wouldn't have to borrow any money), and it would allow her to major in a number of art-related fields that interested her, but it wouldn't give her as broad a liberal arts education as Innercity.

7. *Make the decision*

For many people this is the hardest part. Why? Because of fear, fear that they'll make a bad decision. You can never be 100 percent certain that you're making a good decision. Often it isn't even clear in retrospect. But just remember this: any decision is better than indecision. Even a bad decision is usually better than no decision at all. If Sarah doesn't make up her mind about whether to go to South Moose Falls State College or to Innercity University, she'll wind up going nowhere. If she decides to go to South Moose Falls State College and later considers it a mistake, chances are that she will still find it preferable to not having gone to college at all.

Sarah ended up making a surprise decision. The more she thought about it, the more she realized how important the opportunities at Innercity University were to her. Since it was clear that she couldn't afford it next year, she decided to stay out of college one year and work to save up money so she could go there the following year.

8. *Communicate the decision*

When you are making a decision that affects others, it is extremely important to communicate the decision. Many decision makers make up their minds and keep everyone else in the dark. The decision is useless if it is not communicated. If Sarah doesn't communicate her decision to the college of her choice, she'll end up losing out on a place there.

Sarah sent a letter to Innercity University telling them of her decision. Even though she was no longer interested in South Moose Falls State College, she notified them of that fact too.

MAKING THE BIG DECISION

Now that you've seen how the decision model works, we can return to Mark Fischer's committee. They're moving toward the big decision about where to hold the Sunday school picnic. Since they're using the same decision model, we'll organize the account of their deliberations using the steps of that model.

1. *Define the issue*

As you may remember, the committee narrowed their alternatives to three, so the issue for them is this: will the Sunday school picnic be at the shore, at the state park, or in the Singers' backyard?

2. *List the facts*

The committee discusses a lot of relevant facts, the most important of which are the following:

The park closes at seven in the evening.
The beach will charge thirty dollars for the group.
Renting a bus to go to the beach will cost fifty dollars.
There is a hundred dollars in the budget earmarked for the Sunday school picnic.

3. *Recognize the assumptions*

The committee makes the following assumptions:

More people will come if it's held nearby in the evening than if it's a more distant, all-day affair.

The committee considers this a fairly safe assumption because they know their own preferences and consider themselves representative of the rest of the Sunday school families. They also suspect that was the reason for the poor attendance the previous year.

There will be good weather.

Not too safe an assumption.

People want to swim on a Sunday school picnic.

Again, the committee bases this assumption on their own preferences, but they are less sure of this one. It really comes down to a matter of tradition. There has been swimming at the picnic for as far back as anyone on the committee can remember.

4. *Make estimates*

Somebody has calculated that the food for the picnic will cost about $250 if the Sunday school provides it and that one bus will be sufficient to transport everyone to the picnic. Given that they only have $100 to spend, they add a new fact to their list: the Sunday school can't pay for all the food.

5. *Review goals and long-range plans*

Any of the alternatives will serve the goals and long-range plans of the East Moose Falls Community Church. They'll all provide a time of fellowship. Someone points out that the alternative that will do it best will be the one that attracts the most people.

6. *Analyze alternatives*

The beach sounds pretty good to some of them, but they're afraid that they won't be able to get enough people to come for an all-day event to justify the expense. Since the park closes at seven, it won't allow much time for an evening event. The Singer's backyard has a lot going for it. It's nearby, it won't cost anything if people bring potluck dishes, and it will be easy to reschedule in case of rain (after all, their assumption about fair weather doesn't seem very safe).

7. *Make the decision*

By the time the committee finishes analyzing their alternatives, the decision seems obvious to all of them. They'll have a potluck at the Singer's on the last Friday evening in June.

8. *Communicate the decision*

Mark intends to place an announcement in the church bulletin for the following Sunday and post a sign-up sheet in the lobby a few weeks before the picnic.

Communicating the decision, like so many other aspects of making events happen, becomes more difficult as the planned event itself becomes more complex. The Sunday school picnic decision was easy to communicate—a simple announcement in the bulletin sufficed. It was much harder to communicate the decision about the conference on conferences. To make it clear what was being decided, Julie drew up an outline of the plan to present to the subcommittee for approval.

The subcommittee ended up going with a variation on the first course of action. While that had originally called for a more formal atmosphere, the subcommittee decided on an informal, week-long, unstructured conference in New York.

Julie's outline incorporated many of the documents the subcommittee had generated during the planning phase. It included the following elements:

The purpose

The goals

A draft of the objectives (to be made final just before the event)

The conference theme

The conference dates

The conference location

Keynote speaker possibilities

Major events

An organizational chart for the preparation phase

An organizational chart for the conduct phase

A draft of job descriptions for key positions

Assignments

A tentative budget

A cash-flow plan

Basic and tentative administrative procedures

Now that they've made their big decisions, both Mark's and Julie's committees are done with the planning phase. They're ready now to move forward on the work of preparing for their events.

PREPARATION PHASE

5

ORGANIZING FOR ACTION

> | PREPARATION PHASE |
> | --- |

> | 1. Identifying necessary tasks |
> | --- |

What to write down: Lists of preparatory and conduct tasks.

Selecting a course of action is a big step, but there's still a lot of work ahead before your event can become a reality. If you've ever stayed up all night before some event doing all the last-minute things, you know how true that is.

Why do preparations usually get done at the last minute? And why does the person in charge often get stuck doing most of it? Chances are it's because nobody actually took the time to get organized.

Mark Fischer's planning committee was discussing this very thing. One of the members, Martha Higgins, could remember the year when Jerry Perkins, the superintendent, got called out of town on business the week before the picnic. That was in the days before there was an education committee. Since the Perkinses and the Higginses were good friends, Jerry had asked Martha's husband Bob to fill in for him at the picnic. Bob had said he would, thinking he could referee a softball game as well as the next guy. It turned out Jerry was also putting him in charge of preparations and that none had been made yet. Jerry had been of the "wing it" school. Martha and Bob spent that week running around getting supplies. Then they had to show up at the state park at the crack of dawn to grab tables since Jerry hadn't reserved the group area. It was a chilly morning. As they huddled together sipping coffee and waiting for the fog to lift, Bob had said, "This is ridiculous! There's got to be a better way."

It's obvious that big events need organization, but with simpler events it may not seem necessary. After all, isn't a church supper just a family meal with more people? Who needs to organize that? The truth of the matter is that even a simple family meal takes more organization than you realize. Supper goes smoothly because the preparations for it have been built into your family's life. You not only have a cook, but the kitchen is well-stocked, the guests are all accounted for, and there's a clean-up crew on hand. Much of what you take for granted in a family meal requires careful, deliberate organization in any other event.

The kind of organizing I'm talking about consists of figuring out what needs to be done in what order and then assigning people to do it. Did you ever tell yourself that next time everything is going to be done several days in advance? Was it? If not, maybe it's because you didn't know how to do this kind of organizing. In this chapter you'll learn how.

IDENTIFYING THE WORK THAT NEEDS DOING

The first step in organizing is to figure out what needs to be done. If you did a thorough job of preparing estimates, you should have done most of this already. The question you should have asked yourself then was "What has to be done to make this happen?" Even if you've already done it, ask the question again. Go over the estimate and make any necessary corrections. Check your outline plan too, if you made one. Make sure that you can answer the question, "What has to be done to make this happen?"

As you do this, remember the distinctions we made in chapter 3 between tasks and actions and between preparation tasks and conduct tasks.

A *task* is a unit of work that needs doing. An *action* is one way of accomplishing a task. Let's say we need to get the keynote speaker from the airport to the convention center. That's a task. We can charter a limousine for the day and instruct the chauffeur to pick up and deliver the speaker. That's one possible action. Of course there are cheaper alternatives that will accomplish the same task equally well. We could, for example, ask a friend to drive to the airport and pick up the speaker. In planning and preparation, it will be helpful to distinguish between the task and the action.

Preparation tasks need to be done during the preparation phase to insure that the event will take place successfully. *Conduct tasks* need be done during the conduct phase. Arranging for transportation and speakers are preparation tasks. Picking up the keynote speaker at the train station on the morning of the event is a conduct task.

CLASSIFYING TASKS

The next step is to compile tasks into lists, if you haven't already done this. If you find yourself developing an endless list of necessary tasks, it's probably because you are not being sufficiently general in your statements. "Pick up the coffee, pick up the doughnuts, pick up the sugar, pick up the cream, pick up the tea bags, etc." can be consolidated into "Get supplies for coffee breaks."

Once you have the lists, you can begin the business of classifying and organizing needs. The first breakdown should be between preparation tasks and conduct tasks. Within these two major groups you should distinguish three types of tasks: *primary tasks* that contribute directly to the event taking place, *component tasks* that are essential to the completion of a primary task, and *supplementary tasks* that contribute to the successful realization of a goal but are not essential to the success of the event. Here are some examples. Making a reservation is a primary task. Going to a hotel, filling out a reservation form, and making a deposit are component tasks. Ordering center pieces for banquet tables could be considered a supplementary task.

PRIMARY TASKS

For a small event the primary tasks are few. The Sunday school planning committee decided there were only six.

1. Have families sign up for food to bring.
2. Arrange transportation for those needing rides.
3. Purchase paper plates, etc.
4. Supervise in the kitchen when people show up with food.
5. Organize a game time after supper.
6. Clean up afterward.

For a more complex event, the list of primary tasks should be compiled in writing. Julie Daniels had to do that for the conference. She blocked off a large chunk of time to go over the task lists she had included in the plan outline and to work out a schedule of when each task needed to be done.

COMPONENT TASKS

One of the primary tasks on Julie's list was to make hotel reservations. It, in turn, had three component tasks:

1. Make an initial reservation one year in advance.
2. Make a deposit within ninety days of the event.
3. Confirm in writing the number of conference rooms, guest rooms, and persons expected in attendance at meals forty-five days before the actual conference.

You probably won't have to worry about component tasks if you're organizing a simple event, but you'll find it essential for staying on top of complex primary tasks that are part of a big event.

If a primary task breaks down naturally into several subtasks, then you'll need to make lists to keep track of these component tasks just as Julie did. They may need their own place in the preparation schedule, and you may even assign them to different people. If you're working on an event with lots of other people, you may ask the person assigned to act on the complex primary task to break it down into components and oversee their completion. Whatever the case, successful accomplishment of the primary task will depend on the completion of each of its component tasks.

SUPPLEMENTARY TASKS

Supplementary tasks are not critical to an event. If one or two don't get done, the event will still come off, though it may be less satisfying. On the other hand, if *enough* supplementary tasks don't get done, the success of the event might well be in jeopardy. Planners of a Boy Scout outing, for example, might consider bringing along different kinds of sports equipment. The scouts can make do easily enough without the archery equipment, but if the planners also fail to bring the baseball and basketball equipment and the canoes, the outing is likely to be in trouble.

Supplementary tasks often don't have to be scheduled as tightly as primary and component tasks. The archery equipment, for example, can be picked up several days in advance or just before leaving.

> **PREPARATION PHASE**
>
> > 2. Scheduling preparatory tasks

What to write down: A task-completion schedule.

Once you know what needs to be done, the next thing to do is to get it all organized into a schedule. For this, you'll have to have a good idea of how much time is needed for each required task and how much time is available.

Julie, for example, needed one year to reserve the hotel. If only six months had been available, she would have had to revise some plans. Fortunately, she was working with time to spare. She also had time constraints for other primary tasks related to publicity, registration, and the program, so she had to make sure that there was time available for each of them.

COUNTING BACKWARD FROM THE EVENT

Did you ever notice in those John Wayne movies how the marines were always talking about D day plus two or D day minus three? If D day was going to be March 6, why didn't they just talk about March 3 or March 8? It's so they wouldn't have to reschedule everything if the event was postponed. By planning the time sequence of their tasks in relation to the day of the event, they only had to do the work once.

You should use a similar technique for any event that might be postponed. Again, the complexity of the event and the number of tasks required has some bearing on whether this technique is appropriate. It may be not worth talking about purchasing the food for the Boy Scout outing on event-day minus one, but Julie will have a detailed list of tasks to be completed on event-day minus one even before the conference dates are set.

SEQUENCE-OF-TASKS CALENDAR

For a complex event it is important to develop a sequence-of-tasks calendar. It's like the countdown schedule for the launch of a space shuttle. Figure 5.1 is a sample sequence-of-tasks calendar for a church women's group retreat planned by Mrs. Smith and Miss Peabody. Notice that each task is assigned a completion date in relation to the date of the event.

It may seem like overkill for a church retreat, but as the event grows in complexity so will the need for sequence-of-tasks planning. A simpler event, such as the Boy Scout outing can be handled by listing the primary and supplementary tasks on a calendar as in figure 5.2.

Each primary task should be listed on the sequence-of-tasks calendar. Don't list it at the last date it can possibly be done. Allow enough time in case something goes wrong—like someone getting sick. The primary tasks should also be placed on the calendar at intervals that will be convenient for you to accomplish them.

Important supplementary tasks that must also be accomplished in a specific time frame should also appear on the

Figure 5.1. **Sequence-of-Tasks Calendar: Women's Retreat**

Event day: December 1

Snow cancellation date: December 15

Primary tasks:	Action assigned to:	Accomplishment deadline:		Accomplishment goal:	
		Task sequence:	Calendar:	Task sequence:	Calendar:
1. Reserve campsite	Smith	E -30	Nov 1	E -90	Sept 2
2. Make transportation arrangements	Peabody	"	"	E -45	Oct 17
3. Line up speakers	Smith	"	"	E -60	Oct 2
4. Place announcement in church bulletin	"	E -30	"	E -33	Oct 29
5. Place sign-up list in vestibule	"	"	"		
6. Have pastor announce from pulpit	"	E -20	Nov 11	E -27	Nov 4
7. Check sign-up sheet and finalize number of campsite reservations	Peabody	E -10	Nov 21	E -13	Nov 18
8. Get bank check from treasurer to pay for campsite	Smith	E -5	Nov 26	E -10	Nov 21
9. Confirm all speakers	Peabody	E -4	Nov 27	E -6	Nov 25
10. Pick up materials for coffee breaks	"	E -1	Nov 30	E -2	Nov 29
11. Pick up hymnbooks	Smith	"	"	"	"

October
```
 1  2  3  4  5  6
 7  8  9 10 11 12 13
14 15 16 17 18 19 20
21 22 23 24 25 26 27
28 29 30 31
```

November
```
          1  2  3
 4  5  6  7  8  9 10
11 12 13 14 15 16 17
18 19 20 21 22 23 24
25 26 27 28 29 30
```

December
```
                   1
 2  3  4  5  6  7  8
 9 10 11 12 13 14 15
16 17 18 19 20 21 22
23 24 25 26 27 28 29
30 31
```

Figure 5.2. Sequence-of-Tasks Calendar: Boy Scout Outing

MAY

SUN	MON	TUE	WED	THU	FRI	SAT
		1	2	3	4	5
7	8	9	10 Reserve campground	11	12	13
14	15	16	17	18	19	20
21	22 Pick up archery equipment	23	24	25	26 Buy food	27 Outing
28	29	30	31			

Figure 5.3. **Sequence of Component Tasks: Primary Task #3 — Line Up Speakers**

Event day: December 1 Snow cancellation date: December 15

Component tasks:	Accomplishment deadline: Task sequence:	Calendar:	Accomplishment goal: Task sequence:	Calendar:
1. Establish list of possible speakers			E -110	Aug 16
2. Decide number of speakers needed			"	"
3. Decide among possible speakers			"	"
4. Write invitation to desired speakers			E -100	Sept 2
5. Follow up with phone calls if necessary to get confirmations			E -90	
6. Extend invitations to alternate speakers			E -80	" 12
7. Follow up with phone calls if necessary to get confirmations			E -70	" 22
[3. Line up speakers	E -30	Nov 1	E -60	Oct 2]
8. Send confirmation letters			E -45	Oct 17

```
October
       1  2  3  4  5  6
 7  8  9 10 11 12 13
14 15 16 17 18 19 20
21 22 23 24 25 26 27
28 29 30 31

November
             1  2  3
 4  5  6  7  8  9 10
11 12 13 14 15 16 17
18 19 20 21 22 23 24
25 26 27 28 29 30

December
                   1
 2  3  4  5  6  7  8
 9 10 11 12 13 14 15
16 17 18 19 20 21 22
23 24 25 26 27 28 29
30 31
```

sequence of tasks calendar. Other supplementary tasks may be kept on a list by themselves and done in order as time permits, but you should also calculate the time required to do them. Time gaps between tasks on the calendar are good times to perform these supplementary tasks.

If a primary task requires several component tasks, it might be a good idea to construct a separate calendar for it as shown in figure 5.3.

Notice that Mrs. Smith only set accomplishment goals and not deadlines for component tasks. That's because the deadline really only applied to the primary task itself, but it is conceivable that in some cases you would want to have deadlines for component tasks as well.

Also note that Component Task 8 is listed after the primary task. That's because the action can be delayed without seriously jeopardizing the event.

In this chapter we have emphasized the importance of getting organized before you go into action, but as with everything else, organization can be overdone. Don't let yourself get caught still polishing off your plan on the night before the event. You don't have to wait until the plan is perfected to begin acting. If you have a reasonably detailed plan at this point, it's time to get on with the preparation phase.

6

GETTING DOWN TO WORK

```
┌─────────────────────────────┐
│  PREPARATION PHASE          │
└─────────────────────────────┘
     ┌──────────────────────────────────┐
     │  3. Taking pre-event actions     │
     └──────────────────────────────────┘
```

For me, planning is much easier than doing. Planning is also a lot more fun. Plans can be exactly how you want them to be. Planning things hardly ever causes stress. But doing things—that's work! You are now at the juncture where the doing begins. It's not that planning isn't work too, but now you're faced with deadlines for the first time.

Getting started is a problem for a lot of people. They either don't know where to start, or they find it hard to overcome initial inertia. Once they begin to see themselves making progress, it's easier to keep going. The trick is getting started.

The best way to start is to pick something easy or enjoyable off the sequence-of-tasks calendar and do it. Try to meet your accomplishment goals. If you miss a goal, try to keep the deadline. If you miss the deadline, you may have to make some revisions in your plan.

One important thing to remember is that the character of the event has already been decided. Don't try to redefine the event or change its character at this late stage. That's a sure prescription for disaster.

For a small event, your biggest problem will probably be

yourself. You'll have to exercise the self-discipline necessary to get the work done and fight off discouragement when things are not going the way they should. For a large event, however, several people may have to be involved in taking the actions necessary to "pull off" the event. You'll need to work out a good combination of leaders, followers, and organization.

Each of those elements—leaders, followers, and organization—will be discussed in subsequent chapters. At this point, however, I would like to discuss briefly one very important skill you must have in order to make an event happen if you are working with a large group. This skill is the ability to delegate.

DELEGATING

Delegating is not simply telling someone to do something. Giving orders is not delegating. Delegating means giving people assignments and then allowing them to use their own judgment to figure out how to fulfill them. Asking someone to arrange for the transportation of fifty people from the church to the state park would be delegating. The individual has not been told how to go about arranging for the transportation or what kind of transportation to arrange.

Virtually any task or action can be delegated. The trick is in picking the right person for the job. If a person lacks the requisite skill or the resources to perform a certain task, you may have to give the job to someone else. If, however, he or she merely lacks the necessary authority to do the job, you can usually delegate the authority along with the task. If you ask someone to arrange for the transportation of fifty people from the church to the state park by bus and the bus company requires a $50 deposit, then you'll have to give that person the authority to spend the money.

There is, however, one thing that can't be delegated: responsibility. If you've been appointed to plan a Sunday school picnic, you may delegate the task of arranging transportation and the authority to do it to someone else. If on the day of the picnic, however, it turns out that the individual never arranged for the transportation—guess who is held responsible!

HOW TO DELEGATE

When you are delegating tasks, it's important to provide instructions that communicate clearly what you're asking the person to do. I use the following format in my business and find that it helps minimize misunderstandings and subsequent problems.

1. Give a brief, general description of the job (similar to the statement of purpose described in chapter 2).

2. Delineate guidelines for doing it.
   a. Things that must be done
   b. Things that must not be done
   c. Deadlines and reporting requirements

3. State the name and title of the one to whom the person doing the job is responsible (e.g., you work for me, or you work for Jack).

4. Delegate the authority to do the job (e.g., you may spend money, you may fire someone if necessary).

5. Place limitations on the authority (e.g., you may not incur debts in the name of the organization).

6. Give encouragements to succeed (e.g., state why the task is important).

These instructions, when written, become a job description. They make it possible for the individual to do the job without having to return to you for further clarification and permissions.

DELEGATION PITFALLS

There are two major pitfalls to avoid in delegating. There are probably many other pitfalls, but I will mention just two of them here. Both involve poor styles of leadership: "zero leadership" and "micro-management."

Zero leadership occurs when a leader delegates everything and fails to provide a unified direction. Delegating everything is by no means a bad idea. It is not, as people often think, the sign of a lazy leader. The conductor of an orchestra doesn't play an instrument. He has—appropriately—delegated everything. The problem comes, however, when the conductor sits down to listen to the music rather than standing up and conducting.

Leadership can also be compared to a ship's operations. The captain who delegates everything, or almost everything, or even a lot of things, must provide direction. Without this, the whole organization becomes rudderless, drifting whichever way the wind is blowing at the time. One person may be pushing his own ideas, while another has no ideas to push, and a third is pushing his uncle's point of view. The captain isn't taking charge. That's no way to sail a ship!

The best way to prevent zero leadership is have regularly scheduled meetings at which the leader reminds people of the purpose, goals, and objectives, gets status reports, and generally keeps the project on target.

Micro-management is overmanagement. A leader may delegate tasks without actually letting go of them. Typically this shows up at status report time when the leader gets bogged down in the details of how a task is being performed. Micro-management stifles initiative and is devastating to morale. Moreover, it gets in the way of getting the job done.

You can avoid micro-management by allowing those who work for you to do things their way as long as it is a reasonably acceptable way of doing things. You may consider your way superior, but if you constantly insist on doing things your own way, you end up squelching other people's initiative and consequently their willingness to help. Remember, you can't do it all, so let people help you!

Once again, Mark's committee had it easy—at least in comparison to Julie's subcommittee. With only three primary tasks, they could keep track of things in their heads, and it was simple to divide up the work. Mark said he would coordinate transportation for people who needed rides. Martha Higgins was going to plan the game time. Rachel Singer would take care of the sign-up sheets for food and supervise in the kitchen, calling upon other members of the committee to help her. She was to let someone else know, for example, what they'd need in the way of supplies. Then they'd all stick around and clean up afterward.

Julie's conference will take considerably more work. She'll be dividing the preparation tasks among five or six people over the next year leading up to the conference. Then she'll be coordinating a staff of fifty during the conference itself.

7

"IF ANYTHING CAN GO WRONG, IT WILL"

```
┌─────────────────────────┐
│  PREPARATION PHASE      │
└─────────────────────────┘
    ┌──────────────────────────────┐
    │  4. Planning for contingencies │
    └──────────────────────────────┘
```

What to write down: Contingency plans.

While the planning phase has ended and the character of the event has long ago been decided, there is still some planning that should go on during the preparation phase: contingency planning.

MURPHY'S LAW

We've all heard of Murphy's Law: "If anything can go wrong, it will." The first time you heard it, you may have thought it humorous, but you've probably learned since to recite it as a verbal shoulder shrug. We've come to expect things to go wrong.

Murphy's Law is not always true—in fact, you'll find that most of the time more things don't go wrong than do—but it's true enough to take it into account.

That's where contingency planning comes in.

EXPLORING SCENARIOS

Theoretically, just about anything can go wrong in any situation. For example, a stray moose could wander into the Singers' yard, terrifying everyone, and trampling everything in sight just as the picnickers are settling down to supper. After all, it is East Moose Falls. It's only slightly less probable that the conference on conferences in New York could find itself under siege from a band of roaring Bengal tigers who somehow manage to find their way into the hotel lobby. But since neither of these are really very likely, both groups would do well to develop more realistic scenarios.

Make a list, mental or otherwise, of all the things that could realistically go wrong. There are enough of those: it could rain, the bus could break down, the traffic could be jammed. Then ask which of these are the most likely to happen? Those are the scenarios for which you should have the best contingency plans.

You probably should consider equipment first. Analyze each piece of equipment you're planning to use. Is it likely to break down? Can it be fixed? Are there spare parts or accessories that you should have on hand? Inevitably, the projector bulb will go bad at a very inconvenient time. When it does, the simple, inexpensive precaution of having a spare bulb on hand could save an event.

People have a way of getting sick or otherwise not showing up. Any plan that is dependent on people should have some contingency plans. Usually the keynote speaker shows up, but sometimes he is in an automobile accident at the last minute or becomes deathly sick. What then?

If fair weather is important to the success of the event, you had better have foul-weather plans on hand too.

DEVELOPING CONTINGENCIES

A contingency plan is merely an answer to the question, "What will we do if . . . ?" The answer could be, "Cancel, run, or hide." Those alternatives don't really require any planning, though, so a good contingency should make them unnecessary.

The picnic planners figured they'd just postpone it one week in case of rain. But they could have also come up with an alternate event like going to the West Moose Falls Bible Conference grounds instead, for a game day using the indoor shuffleboard and gym and ending up the day with a huge indoor picnic in the dining room.

DEFINITE DECISIONS

It's tempting to leave contingency plans dangling. You may never have to act on them, so why bother getting too definite? As long as you've given the matter some thought, you won't be caught totally unprepared, right?

If that's what you're thinking, you couldn't be more wrong. Have you ever tried changing horses in the middle of the stream? On the day of the picnic when it starts raining without warning and everyone has a million things to do, that's no time for the committee to resume its discussion on contingency planning.

Even though contingency plans are conditional plans, you should still make definite decisions about them. Decide exactly what you will do if it rains or if the speaker doesn't show up.

Make definite decisions about them, and make sure that those in charge on the day of the event know what they are. Then when things do go wrong, you really will be ready.

SHOT CALLER

The final element of a contingency plan is to designate a shot caller. A shot caller is the one who decides when it's time to activate a contingency plan. In other words, the shot caller decides that it looks like rain or that you've waited long enough for the speaker to show up. In most cases the shot caller will be the event director—especially for big decisions. Decisions for which the effects are less weighty can be delegated.

For complicated events, contingency plans should be written out. The plans do not need to be exhaustive. But if there are a lot of things that could go wrong, then it's helpful to have a written list of plans. Figure 7.1 on the next page is a hypothetical written contingency plan.

BACKING OUT IS TOUGH TO DO

You develop contingencies plans so the event can go on even when things go wrong, but sometimes things go so wrong that the only smart thing to do is back out.

When I first joined the Marine Corps, I was told that marines never retreat, and here I am about to advocate that very thing. What can I say? No matter what we've been taught to think, sometimes it's the right thing to do.

The marines don't retreat because they thinks it's cowardly, and successful military men are quite intolerant of cowards. General George Patton, for example, had strong feelings of this nature and perhaps did not contain them as well as he should have.

I suspect that the strong emotional resistance to retreating comes from the training that makes a soldier capable of suppressing the natural urge to survive and willing to rush headlong into the face of death. It's essential training for a soldier—ironically, it gives him a better chance of surviving—

Figure 7.1. **Contingency Plans**
East Moose Falls Community Church Sunday School Picnic

Scenario	Contingency	Shot Caller
It rains before picnic starts or forecast is more than a 50% chance of rain	Postpone until rain date	Sunday school superintendent
It rains after picnic has begun	Move to West Moose Falls Bible Conference Grounds	''
Bus breaks down anytime before picnic and cannot be repaired	Rent bus from Kid Movers	''
Bus breaks down en route	Bus to be followed by station wagon carrying food, etc. Station wagon can transport drivers back to church to get cars to shuttle everyone to the park	Bus driver

but it makes it hard to retreat. It's too close emotionally to the impulse to run in fear for a trained soldier to handle it well.

So marines don't retreat, but I did learn that one of their most famous successes occurred when they advanced in the opposite direction. During the Korean conflict the First Marine Division found itself surrounded. To their way of thinking they had the Chinese communists right where they wanted them—everywhere. They didn't have to hunt for them. They didn't have to aim—just shoot. Prudence dictated that they advance from the Chosin Reservoir to the seacoast.

This advance had not been in their original battle plan, and it was kind of going back over the same territory, but it was certainly not a retreat. Compared with perhaps the most famous retreat in history, Napoleon's retreat from Moscow, it was a great victory. Napoleon abandoned equipment, wounded men, and whole military units as he fled to Paris in the bitter cold of the Russian winter. When the marines left the Chosin Reservoir, they took their wounded and their equipment with them and they inflicted heavy casualties on the pursuing enemy.

The point of this little digression isn't to acquaint you with Marine Corps history. It is a prelude to saying that there need be no shame in backing out. The shame comes only in the way it is done.

If you lay off your employees without notice, plunge your investors into ruin, and leave ticket holders standing at the door, then it sounds like Napoleon's retreat. But if you can pay off your creditors, help your employees find alternative work, and limit your investors' losses, then it's a little more like the marines advancing from the Chosin Reservoir.

Is backing out always a sign of cowardice and irresponsibility? Absolutely not! Sometimes it's the most responsible course of action. The difficult part is reading the situation correctly. Generally circumstances are ambiguous. It may seem as if moving ahead will lead to certain disaster, and yet you may suspect that the plan of action is sound and that you're just experiencing a failure of nerve.

You need to be able to recognize the signs that it's time to cancel an event. We'll review the Inman model and look at places where telltale indicators might show up.

BACKING OUT IN THE PLANNING PHASE

In the planning phase, the first negative indicators are likely to appear in the preparation of estimates. If all the estimates indicate it can't be done, don't try it. You may want to analyze the estimates more closely to see if they're accurate, or you may want to brainstorm for some new ideas. But you also have some good reasons to call the event off. If the event has little appeal or if the estimates indicate inadequate resources, you will likely meet with failure.

Another point in the planning phase when you might want to consider backing out is when you're defining and developing the purpose, goals, and objectives. You might discover, for example, that the event is really not consistent with the mission of the sponsoring body or that you can't establish objectives that support that mission in any way.

The planning phase is a good time to back out. It's easiest then because you haven't invested much in it yet. Later on there will be more at stake. Indeed, one of reasons for having the planning phase is to assess the feasibility of the event. You don't write the purpose, goals, and objectives and make estimates just to select the best alternative. You also do it to find out if the event makes any sense. If it doesn't, don't try to do it. If the event won't "fly," don't launch it.

BACKING OUT IN THE PREPARATION PHASE

In the preparation phase you may find a good reason to back out or change plans when you're scheduling the preparatory work. You might discover that you just don't have enough time to complete the preparations before the scheduled event. It would have been better if you had caught this when you were making your estimates, but if you didn't, face up to it now.

Later on as you're working on the preparations, missed deadlines or other unforeseen circumstances may force you to cancel or postpone the event. If someone was supposed to acquire reservations at a hotel in Chicago and this turns out not to be possible, then you will need to rethink your plans. If there is time, you may be able to find another hotel. If not, you may have to postpone or cancel. Of course, if you had done good contingency planning, you might have avoided a dilemma like this.

The closer you get to the start of the actual event, the more serious a cancellation becomes. For one thing, it's likely to be expensive. With a large event you may have to forfeit deposits and fees to hotels, caterers, or speakers. At the same time, you may also have to return money to registrants.

BACKING OUT ON THE DAY OF THE EVENT

By the time you're down to the actual day of the event a cancellation is likely to be more like a rout than a retreat. Unless it is absolutely impossible, the best rule of thumb is to go through with the event and do the best you can. At that point carrying on may be less disastrous than cancelling. If there was some foreseeable reason that the event might have to be cancelled at the last moment, you should have a contingency plan developed to prevent such a rout. Now's the time to activate it.

CANCELLATION OR POSTPONEMENT?

The decision to cancel is usually a three-way decision to cancel, postpone, or go through with it. It can even become more complex if you also consider modifying the event.

In any case, it's a decision, so you can use the same decision model developed in chapter 4. At a time when you might be tempted to panic and run, working through the steps of the model can help you keep a calm head for making a sound decision.

1. *Define the issue*

Are you considering canceling, postponing, or modifying the event? Determine what your realistic options are.

2. *List the facts*

Why are you considering these alternatives? List as many reasons as you can think of.

3. *Recognize the assumptions*

What are the indefinable aspects of the decision?

4. *Make estimates*

What will be the cost of each of the possible courses of action?

5. *Review goals and long-range plans*

Do the long-range plans of the organization have a bearing on the decision?

6. *Analyze alternatives*

In view of all the above, what is the best course of action?

7. *Make the decision*

Make a clear and final decision. Do not hedge!

8. *Communicate the decision*

Make sure that everyone who has been involved in the event or who has been made aware of the event is informed of its cancellation, postponement, or modification and that there is an honest, stated reason for the change.

DEALING WITH STRESS AND DISCOURAGEMENT

As you work on an event, there will be times when you are discouraged or feel a lot of stress. These two factors may cause you to want to cancel, when from an objective point of view everything is going fine! We need to review just briefly what causes stress and discouragement and how to combat them. While they are are two very different phenomena, they can be treated similarly.

Discouragement is the feeling that you are failing and cannot succeed. Stress makes you feel panicky. You may fear that you cannot keep your emotional composure, or you may lose it altogether. These are both emotions with which I am personally well acquainted. I am not a physician and do not know the scientific explanations for them, but I know what works for me. Perhaps it will help you as well.

PREVENTION

The best medicine is always preventive medicine. As you come down to the wire, with two days to go and two week's work, it's going to be hard to ward off stress and discouragement.

One way you can prevent them is by scheduling your work better in the first place. Realistic work assignments and schedules with generous allowances for the inevitable complications can go a long way toward making the preparation phase a less stressful and discouraging time for you.

Of course, once you're in the thick of things, that won't help. At that point, you can still work at preventing stress and discouragement by practicing good habits in general. Get your sleep, eat regular meals, exercise regularly, and maintain a balanced schedule of activities.

During the preparation phase, when you are on the run constantly, it is very easy to change your basic life style with the rationale that this is only for a few weeks. But when you change your eating and sleeping habits, grabbing a hot dog here and a candy bar there or pulling all-nighters, you throw off your body's regular functions, and that can effect your general feeling of well being. Medically speaking, I think the jury is still out on these matters, but I find them to be true for me. Stress, discouragement, and life in general are all more tolerable when I eat well, sleep well, and exercise.

FIGHTING DISCOURAGEMENT

If you haven't been able to avoid discouragement, then you have to fight it. One thing that helps is having someone to work with, or failing that, someone to talk to about it. Other people can provide you with the perspective that you lack in periods of discouragement, and they can help you bear the burden.

Another helpful measure is to keep your eye on the goal. Why are you doing what you are doing? What is your purpose? If you keep the goal clearly in mind, it can help you tolerate the confusion and complications and setbacks that lead to discouragement. Remember those World War II movies?

"Tell us again. Why we are doing this?"

"For Mom and apple pie."

FEAR OF FAILURE

One of the major causes of stress and discouragement is the fear of failure. For some reason we in America have been, on the whole, a very successful people. Along with our success we have acquired a strong fear of failure. Perhaps this fear contributes to our success, but sometimes it is also the cause of our failure. Fear of failure can cause us to be too cautious, or it can cause us to back out from discouragement when we could be successful. We need to ask ourselves if we are acting out of a fear of failure or for good, sound reasons.

REMEMBER GENERAL ROBERT E. LEE

General Robert E. Lee could be described as the most admired failure in history. On the face of it, it's hard to see him as anything other than a failure. He lost the war! But we admire General Lee—even us Yankees! Why? Because he maintained his integrity even in failure.

There is a stark contrast between the picture of General Lee standing with General Grant at Appomattox, and the much-publicized scene of a South Vietnamese general committing suicide in front of a military monument. What is that stark difference?

General Lee knew that he had done his best in pursuing the war with the North. As a general, we might say he far out-generaled his opponents. Even if we do not agree with his reasons for pursuing the war, we have to recognize that in his own mind he had fought for what he considered good reasons. He was faced with seeing the men of his army nearly annihilated, and the survivors were certain to suffer grievous wounds, long captivity, and perhaps the permanent loss of property and rights. He knew that, given the alternatives, the decision to surrender was the best possible decision.

For Robert E. Lee, what would cause men of lessor stature lifelong humiliation, became his reason for a place in history. He is the man who saw that all was lost, accepted this fact, and then went on with his life. Of all the generals and politicians of the Confederate States of America it is General Robert E. Lee, standing tall and with unblemished dignity at Appomattox, who is the most remembered leader. I even think when I look at that picture, that General Grant has a slight gleam of jealousy in his eye that anyone else could stand so tall, look so brave, and be so dignified, in General Grant's moment of victory. It's as if General Lee were getting the gold medal and General Grant the silver!

We can learn a tremendous lesson from General Robert E. Lee. We can learn not to fear failure, to do our best, and to accept the consequences.

OUT OF PHASE

8

GOOD LEADERS

This chapter and the next three chapters deal not with a particular phase of event planning, but with certain elements of making an event happen that must be present in every phase. These include good leaders, good followers, good organization, and good decisions.

Some jobs you can do by yourself. Others require some help from friends. Then there are the really big jobs that take an army or something about that size. As a planner, you have to recognize which size you're working with. An event can fail if the person in charge tries to do it all when the job is really too big. Even businesses and organizations fail for the same reason. The wise planner knows how to size up a job and when to call for help.

But knowing when you need help and calling for it isn't enough. You also need to know how to lead.

What exactly makes a person a leader?

There are a lot of positions that can benefit from a person who is a leader. Managers, supervisors, administrators, chairmen, and even military commanders do work for which leadership qualities are an asset, but holding such a position will not necessarily make you leader.

A leader is a person who can get people to do what needs to be done willingly. In other words, a leader is someone who can get others to follow.

Much has been written about what makes a good leader.

The usual approach is to list the requisite traits. Among others, integrity, honesty, enthusiasm, energy, and self-confidence always show up on the list. The problem with that approach is that I know people with all those traits who couldn't lead a cow to water, and you probably do too.

I've decided to come at the question from a different angle. I tried to think about people who have led me, and I asked myself what about them made me willing to follow. I'd like to tell you a couple of military stories about leaders and followers. One is from my own military experience, and the other is from something I read, but they both point to what leadership is all about.

A LESSON FROM LEWIS WALT

When I was a young second lieutenant in the Marine Corps, I heard a lot about leadership, and I saw a lot of leading going on around me.

My first leaders were the drill instructors. They definitely could get recruits to do just about anything. They yelled at us, threatened us, and humiliated us, and we accomplished feats we had never thought possible before. I ran faster and farther, carrying heavier loads than I would ever have thought I could. There were also officers around us, and when they walked by we "gangwayed." We did anything they asked.

We were definitely being led. And we started acting like our leaders—the drill instructors mostly. We polished our brass like them, shined our shoes like them, cut our hair like them. We were becoming leaders like them.

Then one day after we had become second lieutenants, we had a visitor who came to talk to us about leadership. He was General Lewis Walt, a four-star general and veteran of three wars, and he had just returned from Vietnam.

We were called to attention, and General Walt came in wearing his dress blues, every inch of his barrel chest covered with medals. He spoke in a soft voice. "Please be seated, gentlemen." He called us gentlemen, not "maggots!" And he began with these words, "You men are here to become leaders. There is nothing I could tell you which is any more important to being a leader than what Jesus Christ said to his disciples two thousand years ago."

Wait a minute, I thought, is that the chaplain giving the invocation? No, it was General Walt speaking. He continued. "Jesus told his disciples, 'He who would be the greatest among you must be the servant of many.' That is what leadership is all about. If you want to lead marines, you will have to serve them."

General Walt then elaborated on his opening sentence by telling a number of stories from his long and illustrious career. I don't remember many of those actual stories anymore, but I do remember him telling us that the Marine Corps had many traditions which teach that the leader must be the servant.

He alluded to one tradition I had already observed with some curiosity. When hot food is brought to the marines in the field, the officers do not get served until after all the enlisted men have been served. This had always seemed to me the reverse of what it should be, but with General Walt's comments in mind it now made sense. The officers were leading by serving. They were putting the needs of their men before their own.

A LESSON FROM BARON VON STEUBEN

Later I learned that General Walt's ideas were not entirely novel. Nor were they unique to Marine Corps leaders. When George Washington was at Valley Forge, Baron Von Steuben came from Germany to help him train an army. His instructions were published by the Continental Congress. Here are some of his instructions to captains:

A captain cannot be too careful of the company the state has committed to his charge. He must pay the greatest attention to the health of his men, their discipline, arms, accouterments, ammunition, clothes, and necessaries. His first object should be to gain the love of his men by treating them with every possible kindness and humanity, inquiring into their complaints, and when well founded, seeing them redressed. He should know every man of his company by name and character. He should often visit those who are sick, speak tenderly to them, see that the public provision, whether of medicine or diet, is duly administered, and procure them besides such comforts and conveniences as are in his power. The attachment that arises for this kind of attention to the sick and wounded is almost inconceivable; it will, moreover, be the means of preserving the lives of many valuable men.

His instructions to lieutenants were similar:

He should endeavor to gain the love of his men, by his attention to everything which may contribute to their health and convenience; he should often visit them at different hours; inspect into their manner of living; see that their provisions are good and well cooked, and as far as possible oblige them to take their meals at regulated hours. He should pay attention to their complaints, and when well founded, endeavor to get them redressed; but discourage them from complaining on every frivolous occasion.

KEEP THEIR BEST INTERESTS IN MIND

A year after I had heard General Walt speak, I was in Vietnam. There I observed how willing the men were to be led by a lieutenant who seemed to keep their best interests in mind, and how reluctant—nearly mutinous—they were when they had to follow a lieutenant who had only his own career in mind. I tried hard to serve and found that when I looked out for the best interests of my men, they looked out for my best interests as well—one of which was keeping me alive.

Now I know leading the East Moose Falls Community Church Sunday school picnic is certainly a long way from leading marines in combat, and we can hope that conditions will never be as bad as they were at Valley Forge, but the principle is the same. How do you get people to do what you want them to do? You must have their best interests in mind.

Why would anyone help you plan the Sunday school picnic? Because they want it to be a success! Help them realize this goal. Why would anyone help you plan and conduct the conference on conferences? Some will help because they care about the association. Perhaps others will do it because it will look good on their resume or because it will be an opportunity to meet people. Whatever their reasons, they will best help you if you appear concerned for them and what their interests are.

LEADING BY COMMITTEE

So far we have discussed leaders as individuals ignoring the fact that many events are put into the hands of a committee. How does a committee lead? Well, have you heard the joke about the camel? It's a horse designed by a committee.

The fact is that committees often pull in so many different directions at one time that nothing gets done. A committee leads best by reserving powers to itself while delegating the work to individuals. For example, the subcommittee for the conference on conferences gave the work of making estimates to each of the various members but reserved for itself the decision as to which course of action would be taken. In a sense, the committee is not so much leading as it is setting limits and boundaries for the leaders.

As the committee moves from planning to preparation and the event itself, it will likely be necessary for the committee to put a leader in charge. The committee must delegate its work if it wishes to see the work accomplished efficiently. If the committee doesn't appoint an event director and insists on making decisions on every action itself, the event may never take place.

9

GOOD FOLLOWERS

While he was commandant of the Marine Corps, General P. X. Kelley commented on how so many former commandants had written about leadership in their retirement. He said that when he retired he intended to do something different. He would write a book on "followership." He went on to say that marine officers tend to think of themselves primarily as leaders and a lot of emphasis is put on developing and exercising leadership. In thinking back over his own career, however, he noted that he personally had spent most of his career in the role of a follower. He further observed that this was true of most marine officers. In fact, the higher they got in rank the truer it was.

General Kelley started me thinking. He had a good point. A marine always has a boss even when also serving as a boss. That being the case, a marine always has to be somewhat of a follower.

What is true of a marine's work is also true of many civilian careers. People usually spend a lot of time working for someone else. A college dean reports to the college president. A deputy sheriff reports to a sheriff. But it's not just reporting to someone else that makes a person a follower. It's having to support some other decision maker. When someone else is "calling the shots" and you're helping to implement the decision, you're being a follower.

Since all of us spend so much of our lives being followers,

it's important that we consider exactly what makes a good follower. Clearly, followership is a very important ingredient in "making it happen."

FOLLOWERSHIP

I would define followership as the art of helping someone else lead. It's the art of being a good assistant or a good staff worker. Before I elaborate further on the principles of being a good follower, I'd like to tell a few stories about some followers—both good and bad ones.

When I was a young second lieutenant, one very clever way the Marine Corps had of teaching us about leadership was to invite the "experienced led" to talk to us about leadership from their perspective. Four senior staff noncommissioned officers were asked to speak to us. Their assigned topic was to tell us about the best and worst lieutenants they had ever worked for. It was an extremely valuable lecture. I'd like to try it in reverse for you here. I'll tell you about the best and worst staff workers I ever had.

THE WORST OF FOLLOWERS

The worst follower I ever had was Jim, my primary assistant at one point. I've changed his name to protect the incompetent. In fact, Jim is a fictionalized composite of several people. I had inherited Jim from the previous person who held my position, and I was perfectly happy with him throughout my first four months on the job. He was bright, dedicated, productive, self-disciplined, and he knew the position better than I did. He usually did all the routine work, knowing that I was new and would not yet fully understand it.

At about the fourth month I began to grow disenchanted with him. By then I had learned the position and organization well enough to have my own ideas about what needed to be done. Just about that time the quality of Jim's work began to deteriorate. I would give him projects to complete for me and then discover that they were taking longer than expected to complete. Every time I asked Jim about them, he would tell me that they weren't finished yet because he was working on something else that "had" to be done. These were always projects that I considered lower priority. Jim was setting his own priorities, and my work was getting put on the back burner.

About the same time, I noticed something else. All along, Jim had been telling me about this or that problem, and when I suggested a solution, Jim pointed out how that solution wasn't a good one. At first I let this go because Jim had more experience than I. About the fourth month in the position, as I came to understand the problems better, I began to realize that my solutions had been good and that he had exaggerated the problems. Jim was preoccupied with problems, but refused to institute corrective actions that were not of his own devising.

There was another thing that bothered me about Jim. Every time a problem came up in the organization, Jim was very good at analyzing why it had happened, and he always had somebody to blame. He never blamed me directly, but it was always someone I had hired. Sometimes he was right, but even then his insights weren't helpful. What I needed was a solution to the problem rather than a long historical analysis of how it happened and who was to blame.

Jim never did anything serious enough to get fired on the spot. He always backed down from going too far. He always managed to get things done when given a deadline—just before the deadline that is. He worked for me a long time—or rather he worked for himself under my supervision. Finally, I told him he had to go.

Jim had very many good qualities, but he was not a good follower—at least not for me. He was too intent on being his own boss.

THE BEST OF FOLLOWERS

Now let me tell you about Barbara. Barbara is real, but I've changed her name. Technically, she was a secretary, but she was actually more of a co-worker. Barbara was much older than I. She had children almost my age. She was at that age when many young people would have considered her too old to have new ideas. I think at first she was afraid of me, but she was very organized and productive. Despite the fact that she had been working for someone else in the same position, she quickly adapted to changes I wanted to make. She made my priorities her priorities. She even took the initiative to do things I hadn't asked her to do that she knew would fit into my general program. Barbara was always making me look good! Barbara was still working there long after I left.

GREAT FOLLOWERS OF HISTORY

We often think of history as the study of great leaders. Actually history is full of great followers, and we can learn as much from the great followers of history as we can from the great leaders.

William Marshal, Earl of Pembroke

William Marshal was in the service of the kings of England from 1170 to 1219. He served four different kings. He had no legitimate claim to the throne himself, but could easily have seized power on several occasions. Instead, he kept the lawful king in power and served the king and England by conducting an efficient and just administration.

William first achieved reputation as a soldier and statesman under Henry II. When Henry II died and his son Richard the Lion-Hearted came to the throne, William ran England while Richard was away on adventures in the Holy Land and on the continent. Some historians suggest that England fared well in these years largely because Richard was away and William was at the helm.

Richard was followed by his brother John, often regarded as England's worst king. But William Marshal remained loyal to him. When the barons rebelled against John, it was William who stuck with him and advised him that the best course for England was for John to accept the *Magna Carta* that the barons were demanding. In this way William became largely responsible for one of the greatest landmarks of English law.

When John died, his legal successor was still a boy. It was

William Marshal, now seventy years old, who again became the practical ruler of England. As the regent, he reaffirmed the *Magna Carta,* defeated a French attempt to conquer England, and unified a disordered land.

Never once was William Marshal guilty of plotting to ascend to the throne of England. He made England great, by serving its leaders. William did not follow only great leaders. In fact, he served some of England's worst kings. In the end it was England which was the benefactor of the gifts and abilities of this great follower.

George C. Marshall, General of the Army, Secretary of State

Most people think of generals only as leaders, and of course, they are leaders, but General George C. Marshall was even greater as a follower of the leadership of President Franklin D. Roosevelt. The great battlefield generals of World War II would never have been heroes, if Marshall had not been an even greater follower.

I am sure Marshall would have much preferred to have had a field command. He had been to the field in the Philippines, during World War I, and in China, but when World War II broke out he was sitting behind a desk in Washington as the Chief of Staff of the United States Army.

Marshall's accomplishments are astonishing. He raised the strength of the army from 200,000 (smaller than today's Marine Corps) to over 8 million. He changed the theory for deployment of tanks and saw to the creation of sixteen armored divisions. He phased out horse cavalry, coastal artillery, and horse-drawn artillery. The field artillery was upgraded from 75mm. guns to 105mm. guns. The modern American army concept of deployment, which eliminates regiments in favor of self-contained battalions, began under Marshall in the new armored divisions. The army air corps became an air force in all but name. Airborne divisions came into existence. Most amazing of all he created a logistics system to support this gigantic, far-flung, mechanized army. Napoleon was not able to supply his army in Moscow from France, but Marshall supplied his army in Germany, Italy, North Africa, Alaska, the South Pacific, South East Asia, China, and greatly assisted in the equipping of the armies of England, France, and Russia.

This man did not lead on the battlefield, but he is one of the greatest heroes of World War II, because he stayed in Washington and followed!

CHARACTERISTICS OF A GOOD FOLLOWER

Against the backdrop of all these examples, I think we can now state some general principles about what good followers should be like. I'll list them in the form of advice to followers.

1. Be a team player. Put the success of the event above your own, and work for that success.
2. Recognize the rightful authority of the leader. Your job is to help the leader bring off the event.
3. Make the leader's priorities yours. Remember the event has already been defined. Do not spend your time trying to redefine the event.
4. Take initiative in achieving the leader's goals. You don't always have to wait for instructions to do the obvious.
5. Do the job you have been assigned rather than what you think the job ought to be.
6. Assume you are responsible for all matters relating to your assignment unless you have specifically been told something is not your responsibility.
7. Do complete work.
8. Don't meddle in what the leader is giving others to do.
9. Finally, remember that we are all followers doing God's work. Satan's fall seems to have had something to do with wanting the boss's job.

10

GOOD ORGANIZATION

We have defined leadership as the ability to get people to do what needs to be done willingly, and we have said that the best leaders are the ones who lead by serving their followers. That is all true, of course, but we've oversimplified the picture by reducing it to people: leaders and followers. Leaders need to work with followers in an organization.

Organizing is a matter of giving structure to things. Organizing a project or an event is a matter of matching up people and tasks within a structured working relationship. Once you have more than a couple of people working together, you need to consider how to organize yourselves.

TASK-ORIENTED ORGANIZATION

Some people start organizing by looking at the people and trying to figure out who can do what. They might say, "Sally can type. Let her type the programs. Joe is strong. Let him do the lifting. Alice is good looking. She can be the receptionist. John, what can John do?" Aside from being sexist, that approach just won't work well. You would find you had more expertise in some areas than you need and not enough in others.

A much better approach is to start with the tasks and find the right people to do them! Start by looking at what has to be done. Then group together tasks that require similar talents. After the tasks have been grouped, put someone in charge of each group. Then give the ones in charge enough people to do the work. Finally, each of the group leaders should go through the same process for their groups, forming subgroups for each task and putting someone in charge of each. That's how it is done in successful businesses and organizations.

CLASSIC ORGANIZATIONS

You need not start from scratch when you want to organize tasks. The same groupings of tasks occur again and again in organizations. Among them are tasks related to finances, marketing, administration, and logistics. These common groupings have resulted in classic divisions of labor that are repeated from organization to organization. Chances are you can use these same classic divisions of labor—with some modifications—in your particular situation.

Most people are familiar with the classic organization of democratically run groups that have an elected president, vice president, secretary, and treasurer. While it is an acceptable organization for most purposes, conducting an event usually calls for many tasks that do not readily fit these categories.

The military provides us with another model. The typical, battalion, regiment, or division in one of the branches of the armed forces has the kind of structure shown in figure 10.1.

Figure 10.1. **Battalion Staff**

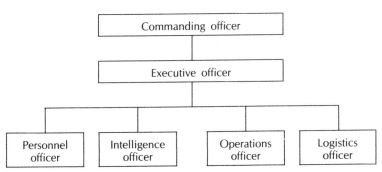

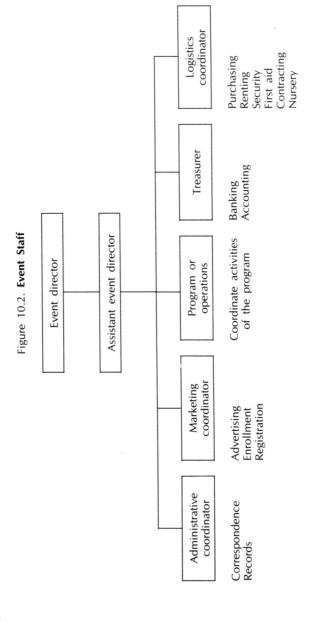

Figure 10.2. **Event Staff**

This structure provides for the even distribution of the typical work load among staff members of a military unit. The various functions are almost self-explanatory. The commanding officer is the boss. The executive officer is his primary assistant and functions as boss in the absence of the commanding officer. The personnel officer is responsible for keeping track of people and their problems and is often assisted by an administrative officer who keeps track of the paper work. The intelligence officer is responsible for keeping the commanding officer informed of what everyone else is doing—friends and foes, the weather, and anything the commanding officer deems essential information. The operations officer usually puts together plans and coordinates the execution of the plans. The logistics officer is responsible for supplies, ordinance, motor vehicles, food, water, and whatever else is needed.

Theoretically this same organization could be used for any operation, civilian or otherwise, but it too would need some adapting. For one thing most operations don't need an intelligence officer. For another, it leaves out some very common tasks. Since military units don't keep their own financial records and are never engaged in sales, their organization doesn't include structures for handling those tasks.

If the democratic model is too simple, the military model is probably too complex. What we need is a simple framework that could also suffice for most complex events, as suggested in figure 10.2. Use the positions you need and ignore the rest.

The simpler the event, the less complex the organization needs to be. It could, for example, be as simple as figure 10.3.

Figure 10.3. **Simple Event Staff**

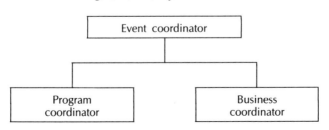

ORGANIZATIONAL PITFALLS

Avoid tall, broad, lopsided, and snarled structures. Figures 10.4 through 10.7 show what these are like. Each diagram looks different. What they all illustrate, however, are organizations in which the structure is out of control. No matter how big your staff gets—and make sure you really need that many people— keep the lines of authority clear and manageable.

JOB DESCRIPTIONS

Delineating the organization, is only half of the work of organizing. Once you've grouped the tasks and decided who will do .what, these individuals need specific written instructions. In chapter 6 we discussed delegating and described delegating instructions. Such instructions, when committed to writing, form a job description. The following is recommended as a guide to writing a job description. Notice its similarity with the suggested outline for delegating instructions.

Format for a job description

1. Job title

2. A brief, general description of the job (similar to the statement of purpose described in chapter 2)

3. Guidelines for doing it
   a. Things that must be done
   b. Things that must not be done
   c. Deadlines and reporting requirements

4. Person and position to whom the individual with this position is responsible (e.g., the administrative clerk reports to the administration coordinator)

5. Authority (e.g., the administrative clerk may make expenditures of twenty dollars for office supplies within the budget allotment)

Figure 10.4. **Broad Organization**

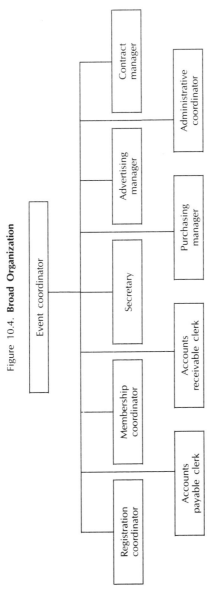

Can the event coordinator coordinate all the coordinators? Notice that everyone reports to the main person!

Figure 10.5. **Tall Organization**

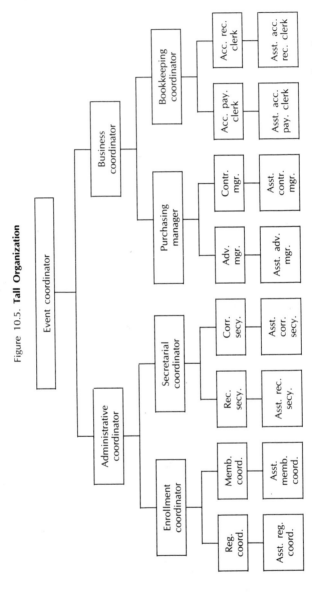

How long will it take for a suggestion to get from the assistant recording secretary to the event coordinator?
Are all these intermediate levels necessary?

Figure 10.6. **Lopsided Organization**

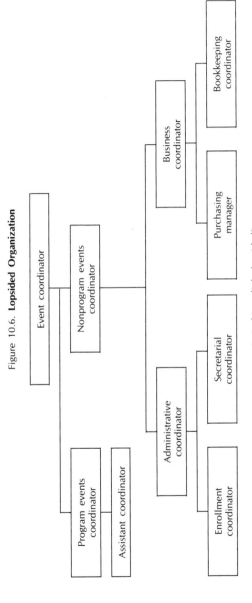

Isn't this a little lopsided?

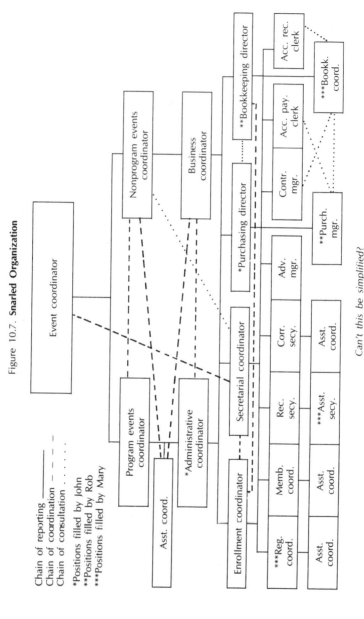

Figure 10.7. **Snarled Organization**

Chain of reporting ——————
Chain of coordination – – – –
Chain of consultation . . . . . .

*Positions filled by John
**Positions filled by Rob
***Positions filled by Mary

Event coordinator

Nonprogram events coordinator

Business coordinator

Program events coordinator

*Administrative coordinator

Secretarial coordinator

Enrollment coordinator

Asst. coord.

*Purchasing director

**Bookkeeping director

Adv. mgr.

Contr. mgr.

Acc. pay. clerk

Acc. rec. clerk

**Purch. mgr.

***Bookk. coord.

Corr. secy.

Rec. secy.

Memb. coord.

***Reg. coord.

Asst. coord.

***Asst. secy.

Asst. coord.

Can't this be simplified?

110

6. Limitations on authority (e.g., you may not incur debts in the name of the organization)

7. Pay and benefits

PRINCIPLES OF SOUND ORGANIZATION

We may summarize what we have said in this chapter by stating six principles of sound organization.

1. *Unity of responsibility.* Each person should report to one and only one supervisor.
2. *Homogeneity of tasks.* The tasks assigned each person should be similar in nature.
3. *Authority commensurate with responsibility.* Each person must be given the authority to make the decisions necessary to do the tasks he or she has been assigned.
4. *Equitable work distribution.* All workers on a particular level should have relatively equal workloads.
5. *Workable subordinate/superior ratio.* The number of persons assigned to one supervisor must not be greater than that supervisor is able to supervise effectively. Avoid tall, broad, lopsided, and snarled structures.
6. *Job descriptions.* Provide clear, concise, and written job descriptions.

11

MORE ON DECISION MAKING

Much has been written about the decision-making process. Some universities even have departments of decision science. As with any area of science, you don't need to know everything about the theory of decision making to actually make decisions, and yet there are some principles from decision-making theory that can help you make better decisions.

Throughout this book we've encouraged the use of a decision model. It outlines a process for working toward sound decisions. In this chapter we will look at the larger context in which decisions are made. We will deal with issues such as who has the authority to make decisions, how authority can be delegated, and what hierarchy of decisions an organization faces.

AUTHORITY FOR DECISION MAKING

Before an organization can make decisions, it needs to know who has the decision-making authority. Corporations have charters that legally grant that authority to certain bodies within the organization. They may confer it on the stockholders or the board of directors. Nonprofit corporations may give it to their members. A church's constitution may assign the decision-making authority to a board of trustees, elders, or deacons or to the congregation as a whole.

Whether that body is the board of directors, the church

elders, or the members as a whole, it is the only body with any legal authority to make decisions for the organization In a small organization it may also be the *only* body making decisions. In most organizations, however, that is not the case. Instead, many decisions are left to individuals or committees. A secretary may decide when it's time to buy paper and how much. The treasurer may pick a color for the new checks and decide when to make deposits. The entertainment committee may select the menu for the social event.

As long as the legally constituted body makes all an organization's decisions, there can be no question of authority, but that's just not practical for most organizations. It is inconceivable, for example, that the board of directors of a large organization planning a large event can make decisions about all the details connected with that event. It just doesn't make sense. So the question arises. How can authority invested in the board (or whatever the body is called) be transferred to others in the organization? What's called for is a system of derived or delegated authority.

DELEGATING AUTHORITY

When an organization's workload grows too large for one body to do it all, it must find ways of distributing its work to others in the organization. Similarly, when the organization grows to the point where one body can't make all the decisions, it must learn to delegate decision-making authority.

Authority should be delegated in the same way that tasks are assigned. In fact, the authority to do the work assigned ought to accompany such assignments. If a body is willing to delegate work to others, it must also be willing to give them the authority to make the decisions necessary to do that work.

In the last chapter we discussed organizational structures and lines of authority. An organization's lines of authority should be clearly spelled out and documented so it is clear who has authority for what and who is accountable to whom.

Often new organizations don't formalize decision-making authority. They may just assume, for example, that people will see what needs to be done and do it. Such casual approaches can work for a time when an organization is young, but as it matures, it needs more clearly defined lines of authority. When conflicts arise—and they inevitably do—it helps to have a clearly defined structure to fall back on. Without such a structure there is no way to maintain accountability.

Accountability may seem like a heavy word with connotations of criminal charges and lawsuits. We may think that among fellow church members we don't need it, that we can just operate on trust. If we think that, we're forgetting our own fallen natures. Defining lines of authority and accountability is the responsible thing to do because it provides checks and limits and makes people answerable for what they do.

There's also another good reason for it. We live in a lawsuit-plagued society. While it's tempting to blame it all on greed and a mentality that is quick to sue, institutional irresponsibility has something to do with it too. When organizations don't bother to define lines of authority, they are acting irresponsibly in a way that leaves their decision makers vulnerable to lawsuits.

A HIERARCHY OF DECISIONS

When we're dealing with derived or delegated authority, we can organize decisions into a hierarchical structure that reflects the structure of the organization. Different types of decisions have different ramifications and generally take place at different organizational levels.

The decisions that affect an organization can be about either doctrine, policies, or procedures.

DOCTRINES

An organization can make its own policies and procedures, but it may be limited in what it can do by doctrinal decisions established from above. All kinds of organizations have doctrines. The church certainly does, and so does the military. No one can decide that the Sunday school picnic will include a lamb sacrifice for the sins of the people. Church doctrine excludes it. Similarly, no one can decide to keep the marines on the ships and send the sailors to storm the beaches. Military doctrine insists that it be the other way around.

Other kinds of organizations have their doctrine too. Directors of nonprofit organizations cannot profit from the organization. Corporations chartered to be educational institutions cannot be travel agencies instead. We can define doctrine as that which cannot be changed by anyone in the organization, but only by a legally constituted authority given the power to do so (such as a legislature or a board of directors). Doctrine must be recognized by all, and all an organization's decisions must stay within the constraints of doctrine.

POLICIES AND PROCEDURES

Policies and procedures, on the other hand, can be established within the organization. Policies are broad guidelines set by the highest decision-making body of the organization. Procedures are the ways in which the policies will be implemented and decisions about them can be made at lower levels in an organization.

Consider the decision that all contracts for more than a thousand dollars must be submitted for three bids. It is a policy decision and has implications for all an organization's other decisions about spending money. Both the decision to buy fifty dollars worth of paper and the decision to award a $50 million contract are procedural decisions. One is certainly weightier than the other, but what makes them both procedural is the fact they are implementations of same policy.

Here are three policy decisions and some related procedural decisions.

Policy: All contracts for more than a thousand dollars must be submitted for three bids.
Procedure: Office supplies will be bought from Jones office supply.

Policy: No one will be admitted to membership who does not agree with the organization's statement of purpose.
Procedure: Prospective members may obtain a copy of the statement of purpose from the secretary.

Policy: The general director cannot spend any money in excess of what has been provided for in the budget.

115

Procedure: The budget will be established at the May meeting and distributed by the treasurer.

An organization can use these concepts—the concept of lines of authority and the concept of a hierarchy of decisions—to do its work more effectively. A board of directors bogged down in the details of procedural decisions can learn how to delegate to others and concentrate on making broader policy decisions. An organization that finds itself remaking the same decisions hundreds of times can learn to establish policies that settle the larger questions and provide guidelines for the smaller ones.

CONDUCT PHASE

12

THE EVENT AT LAST

```
CONDUCT PHASE

1. Executing the plan
```

STICK TO THE PLAN

At last the big day has arrived and the event is about to begin. There will be surprises. Count on it. Things will certainly go wrong, even things that your contingency plans don't cover. People will come up to you with last-minute suggestions for changes in the plan. You may have misgivings and think of some changes of your own. But no matter what happens, keep this one thing in mind: *you must stick to the plan!* Changes to the plan at this stage are sure to create problems.

PROBLEMS WITH NO CONTINGENCIES

Despite all the careful planning, the chances are good that you will run into a problem for which you don't have a contingency. I remember assisting with the security for the mammoth bicentennial air show at Willow Grove Naval Air Station in Pennsylvania in 1976. A problem showed up shortly after the show got started. To our surprise, some people tried to leave early. The plan for traffic flow and parking was based on the assumption that everyone would stay for the entire show. It called for traffic to enter as the show began and continue to enter until the show was about half over, after which it would begin exiting. When people started to leave early while others were still arriving, we had a major traffic snarl on our hands. We had to come up with a spur-of-the-moment plan to let them get out. We had to map out an automobile route, set up traffic control personnel, and begin directing traffic—all of which was a major undertaking.

When major modifications such as this have to take place, it's wise to remember the model for decision making.

1. Define the issue
2. List the facts
3. Recognize the assumptions
4. Make estimates
5. Review goals and long range-plans
6. Analyze alternatives
7. Make the decision
8. Communicate the decision

Work through this mentally by yourself or go over the steps with a small group of assistants. You probably have to make a fast decision, but it doesn't have to be rash. Use the model to arrive at a sound decision.

CONDUCT PHASE

2. Supervising the event

Once the day of the event arrives, the most important job of the person in charge is to supervise. Supervision involves giving someone a job to do and then checking to see that it is done. It's not enough to hand out assignments. You must also check—without nagging or being overbearing—to see that they are completed. It will help if you've prepared a checklist of conduct tasks beforehand.

When things go wrong because someone didn't do his or her job properly, it's tempting to blame the person who should have done it, but very often the problem is that the supervisor didn't make it clear what was to be done, when, and how.

A supervisor's instructions should always be as complete and clear as possible and should include the following elements:

1. A general statement as to what the worker is to do (the mission)

2. Guidelines for doing it
   a. What the worker is specifically to be sure to do
   b. What the worker is must not do
   c. When the worker is to be done
   d. What the worker is to do when done, or if he fails to complete the work

3. Clear lines of responsibility (e.g., you work for me, or you work for Jack)

4. Encouragement for the worker's success

I'll be the first to admit that if you really do use this format for every set of instructions it could sound rather ludicrous, but often for even the simplest task all these elements are necessary. Here's an example of how the instructions could be given for a simple assignment to take out the trash.

1. John, the trash cans are getting full. Please empty them.

2. a. Make sure that you:
      1) Empty out *all* the trash, and
      2) Return the trash cans.
   b. Please do not:
      1) Spill the trash on the way to the dumpster, or
      2) Bang up the trash cans.
   c. You must be finished by five this afternoon.
   d. You must come back here when you are finished, or come back here if for any reason you can't finish.

3. Remember that you work for me, but I work for Jack.

4. Please remember how important it is to keep the trash cans emptied out so the place looks neat for the conference participants. Besides, emptying them now should save extra work later on.

Remember, as a supervisor, you should never hesitate to state the obvious. You'll find that what is obvious to you may not be at all obvious to someone else.

Notice that in giving instructions I used the word *please*. Some people think that supervisors should not say "please." They think that if you say it, your workers will think that they are in a stronger position than you and that they don't have to do the work. People who make such excuses for not saying "please" are probably weak supervisors who don't know how to handle people. If you have people working for you who don't respond positively to "please," they shouldn't be working for you.

CHECKING UP

Once you have given the instructions, check to see that the work was done as requested. Make sure you get around so you can see how things are going. Be ever-present. Instead of asking people if they did their work, ask them if they had any problems with it.

When something has gone wrong, one of the most frequent responses made is "I assumed so and so was going to do such and such." Because of this, many supervisors instruct their people to assume nothing. I prefer to state the matter differently. We must assume, but tell them to assume the opposite: no one else is going to do it, so they had better.

In fact, if a supervisor discusses something with you, make these assumptions:

1. When you come across a detail in your job that needs doing, assume it's your responsibility unless you were specifically told someone else was doing it.
2. If someone discusses a job with you, assume that you are being asked to do it. You can help to eliminate ambiguities by concluding such conversations with this question, "Is there something specific you are expecting me to do?"

Sometimes, if the work is distasteful, supervisors try to avoid coming right out and asking someone to do it. Instead of saying, "Please empty the garbage cans," they may try hinting: "Those garbage cans sure could stand to be emptied." Such hinting is a very poor substitute for supervision. If you want someone to do the work, be direct about it.

MICRO-MANAGEMENT

We have been stressing the importance of thorough supervision, but you should also be careful to avoid oversupervising. We discussed the dangers of micro-management briefly when we were talking about delegating. What we said applies equally to supervision. I don't know who coined the term *micro-management* as a derogatory term for how some supervisors operate, but it's a good one. It refers to a style of supervision that is very burdensome and discouraging to subordinates.

Micro-management is overmanagement. It is giving workers something to do and then spelling out the details so minutely as to prevent subordinates from exercising any judgment of their own. In a worse form it is giving subordinates work to do and then jumping on them because they don't do it exactly the way you would have done it.

To avoid micro-management, learn to accept acceptable work even though you could have done better yourself. Learn that there are several ways any job can be accomplished and the way someone else does it may be every bit as good as yours.

```
┌─────────────────────────────┐
│       CONDUCT PHASE         │
└─────────────────────────────┘
        ┌──────────────────────────────────┐
        │  3. Executing  contingencies      │
        └──────────────────────────────────┘
```

When it becomes necessary to execute a contingency plan, follow the same advice given for executing the original plan: *stick to the plan.* Be committed to the concepts behind the contingency plan. Don't try to rethink the whole thing now. Making changes now will defeat the whole purpose for having the plan in the first place. Chances are you'll only make things worse.

Finally, when everything seems to be going wrong, sit down, take out this book, and read the latter part of chapter 7 again. Remember: keep the purpose, goals, and objectives in mind, do the best you can, and don't fear failure.

CONDUCT PHASE

4. Taking post-event actions

What happens when the event is over? Everyone sits down amid mounds of garbage and uneaten hors d'oeuvres and breathes a long sigh of relief. Right? Wrong. At least that's not how it should go. The mark of a truly well-planned and executed event is that people keep working when the event is over. In fact, there should be a renewed burst of activity as everything is cleaned up, packed up, and put away. Only then should the celebrating start. Even after that there is still more work. There will be final bills to pay, and you should have a final meeting of the staff to review the lessons learned from the whole undertaking.

One of the most helpful sources of information I obtained as a young marine lieutenant on my way to Vietnam was a publication entitled *Lessons Learned From Combat Operations in Southeast Asia*. I think there are many people who could profit from a few pamphlets with titles like "Lessons Learned from the East Moose Falls Community Church Sunday School Picnic" or "Lessons Learned from the Conference on Conferences of the American Association of Conference Managers."

Remember: "Those who do not learn from history are destined to repeat it."

EPILOGUE

Both the Sunday school picnic and the conference on conferences turned out well. I was tempted to say that they went off without a hitch—after all, they were planned and organized by the book—but that only happens in stories. In real life, events never go exactly according to plan, and plans are never without flaws. Still, in terms of their goals and objectives, both events were successful.

If anything, the Sunday school picnic was too successful. They had more people than they expected—about 120—and big as the Singer yard was, things were cramped. Nobody seemed to mind, but when the committee talked about it as they were cleaning up, the consensus was that they needed a bigger place next time. They also thought that if they had it to do over again they would have organized the food differently. A potluck with that many people placed a strain on the kitchen. They thought they would have been better off going with hamburgers and hot dogs for everyone.

The conference on conferences was also well attended. The planners exceeded their objective of 20 percent nonmembers. In fact, nearly 30 percent of those attending were nonmembers, and a majority of them joined the ACCM before the conference was over.

House Bill 106 was a big issue at the conference. Among conference managers there was strong opposition to this attempt to regulate conferences, and members pledged enough money to keep a lobbyist in Washington for the next congressional session, long enough, they thought, to lay the bill to rest once and for all.

People seemed to like the new format with more workshops, fewer plenary meetings, and more time to interact informally. When Julie's subcommittee had a chance to review the evaluation sheets filled out by conference attenders they found them overwhelmingly favorable. That matched their own impressions too. Julie had spent a lot of time circulating among the workshops, getting a feel for how things were going, and she sensed that people seemed more relaxed, less harried than in previous years.

The one persistent complaint came from midwesterners and West Coast participants, and there were more of them this year than ever before. Understandably, they all wanted to move the conference to their own cities. Julie suspected they'd be meeting in a different location next time.

APPENDIX

A QUICK-REFERENCE GUIDE
TO THE INMAN MODEL

This quick-reference guide summarizes the contents of the entire book. You can use it as a reminder of the steps to follow to make an event happen.

Like the book, the guide is organized around the three phases of the model—planning, preparation, and conduct—each of which contain a number of distinct stages. It provides a brief description of each stage and, where appropriate, samples of documents associated with the stage.

> **PLANNING PHASE**

> 1. Receiving the mission

What to write down: A description of the mission.

It all begins here. Someone asks you to be in charge of making something happen, you accept, and suddenly you have a mission.

It's important in this stage to make sure that you know exactly what you're being asked to do. Now's the time to eliminate ambiguities by asking for direct and explicit instructions. You also want a clear understanding of the authority you

THE INMAN MODEL FOR MAKING IT HAPPEN

PLANNING PHASE

1. Receiving the mission

2. Establishing the purpose, goals, and objectives

3. Exploring courses of action

4. Preparing estimates

5. Selecting a course of action

PREPARATION PHASE

1. Identifying necessary tasks

2. Scheduling preparatory tasks

3. Taking pre-event actions

4. Planning for contingencies

CONDUCT PHASE

1. Executing the plan

2. Supervising the event

3. Executing contingencies

4. Taking post-event actions

have to carry out the mission. If you can't get them, write a description of what you understand them to be and get it approved by whoever is giving you the assignment.

Elements of a description of a mission:

> The job title (e.g., conference manager)
> The name of the event and a brief description of it
> Specific requirements for the event
> Accountability (i.e., to whom to report)
> The authority of the person in charge
> Limitations on that authority
> Pay and benefits, if any

PLANNING PHASE

> 1. Establishing the purpose, goals, and objectives

What to write down: A statement of purpose.
A list of goals
A list of objectives

You know what you've been asked to do. Now you need to reflect on the point of it all. Why put on the event? Once you know the answer to that, you'll be in a better position to give shape to it.

The stage really involves three separate processes.

Start with the purpose. Try to put into one simple sentence the reason for having the event.

Next, define the goals for the event. The goals should follow from the purpose and amplify it. They're what you hope to accomplish by having the event.

Finally, state the objectives. The objectives should follow from the goals. They are specific, measurable results that will indicate whether or not you have met your goals.

The following diagram illustrates the way the purpose, goals, and objectives are linked.

Purpose, Goals, and Objectives

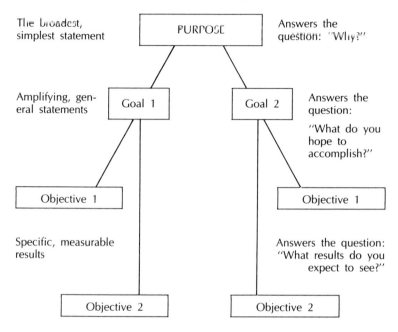

A sample statement of purpose for a conference on conferences:

> The purpose of the twenty-third annual conference on the conduct of conferences is to promote professionalism among conference managers.

A sample list of goals for the conference on conferences:

> Goals for the twenty-third annual conference on the conduct of conferences

> 1. To increase awareness of the role professional conference managers can play in helping business and industry conduct conferences more efficiently and with greater success

> 2. To provide for informal social interaction between the members of the current organization

> 3. To increase the membership of the current organization

4. To establish the mechanism for obtaining the services of and funding a federal lobbyist

A sample list of objectives for the conference on conferences:

Objectives for the twenty-third annual conference on the conduct of conferences

Regarding Goal 1

1. To make sure that at least 10 percent of the attendees are not conference managers, but are executives of corporations or organizations which could make good use of a professional conference manager

2. To have workshops on how the professional conference manager can save business and industry money and get better results

3. To provide a directory of professional conference managers to all conference attendees

Regarding Goal 2

1. To provide at least three social functions of varying formality

2. To provide coffee breaks and meals in a manner that will encourage informal conversation and group interaction

Regarding Goal 3

1. To include among the conference attendees 20 percent nonmembers

2. To sign up as new members 50 percent of the nonmembers attending the conference

Regarding Goal 4

1. To conduct a workshop on House Bill 106 several times during the conference

2. To get 100 percent of the membership to attend a session of the workshop on House Bill 106

3. To obtain from members of the association a resolution regarding hiring a lobbyist

---

PLANNING PHASE

3. Exploring courses of action

What to write down: A list of alternatives.

Once you know *what* you hope to accomplish, you need to start thinking about *how* you can accomplish it. What are your options? Think about some of the possibilities and then narrow down the list to a few of the most promising ones.

A sample list of alternatives for the Sunday school picnic:

1. An all-day picnic at the shore on a Saturday
2. An all-day picnic at the state park on a Saturday
3. A Friday-evening potluck and pool party in the Singers' backyard

> **PLANNING PHASE**

> 4. Preparing estimates

What to write down: Formal estimates.

Now's the time to look more closely at the most promising courses of action that you considered in the last stage. You want to be able to pick the very best one. To do that you need to ask some questions about each one:

Who will it benefit?
How much work is involved?
How much will it cost in money and other resources?

The answers to these questions constitute an estimate. You may also want to prepare—either as part of your estimate or in addition to it—a budget for the event and a cash flow plan.

A sample format for a written estimate:

I. *The benefits.* What are the expected benefits of this course action?
  A. *The appeal.* What appeal does this course of action have?
    1. How many will attend?

    2. Who will attend and what is important about them: ages, sex, attitudes, values?

    3. What are their reasons for attending?

    4. How satisfied will they be with this course of action?

  B. *The accomplishments.* How well will this course of action accomplish the purpose, goals, and objectives of the event?

II. *The work.* How much work is involved?

  A. *Necessary tasks.* What tasks are essential to the success of this course of action?

    1. *Conduct tasks.* Tasks to be done during the event or after its completion.

    2. *Preparation tasks.* Tasks to be done before the event.

  B. *Supplementary tasks.* What optional tasks might improve the quality of the event?

III. *The resources.* What resources will it take to fulfill this course of action?

  A. *Manpower.* How many people will it take?

    A written manpower estimate (see ch. 3) should take the form of a list to evaluate personnel in terms of full-time employees or decimal equivalents.

    1. For necessary tasks (conduct tasks, preparation tasks)

    2. For supplementary tasks (conduct tasks, preparation tasks)

  B. *Materials.* What things are needed?

  C. *Finances.* How much will the event cost?

    Summarize the cost in the estimate and supplement it with a budget and a cash-flow plan.

  D. *Physical.* What facilities are needed?

PLANNING PHASE

5. Selecting a course of action

You've reached the moment for the big decision. If you have estimates for each of your alternatives, you should know what each one has to offer and what it will cost. Now you have to settle on one.

Whenever you have to make a decision, you should go

about it systematically. The following model for making decisions is a good one to use as a guide. Notice that the first five steps bear strong similarities to the steps you've already completed.

Notice too that the final step is to communicate the decision. For a Sunday school picnic that might mean putting an announcement in the church bulletin. The conference on conferences, a much more elaborate undertaking, would require a formal written document. You'll find a list of the elements that should go into such a document below. You'll recognize many of these too. They're based on documents generated earlier in the planning process.

A model for making decisions:

1. Define the issue
2. List the facts
3. Recognize the assumptions
4. Make estimates
5. Review goals and long-range plans
6. Analyze alternatives
7. Make the decision
8. Communicate the decision

What to write down: An outline of the plan for the event.

A list of elements to include in an outline of a plan:

The purpose
The goals
The objectives
The date of the event
The location of the event
Event highlights
An organizational chart for the preparation phase
A draft of the job descriptions for key positions
Names of people assigned to key positions

A tentative budget

A cash-flow plan

Basic and tentative administrative procedures

| PREPARATION PHASE |

| 1. Identifying necessary tasks |

What to write down: Lists of preparatory and conduct tasks.

Once you've decided what you're going to do, you're ready to start preparing for it. Begin by identifying the work that needs to be done both prior to the event (preparation tasks) and during and after the event (conduct tasks). If you made thorough estimates, much of this work may already be done.

For more complex events you may need to make additional distinctions. For example, you can further divide tasks into primary tasks (major tasks that are essential to the success of an event), component tasks (simpler tasks that contribute to the accomplishment of complex primary tasks), and supplementary tasks (tasks that will improve the quality of an event but are not essential to its success).

Remember, you're dealing with tasks at this stage, not actions. A task is a job that needs doing. An action is one way to do the job. Getting the keynote speaker from the airport to the hotel is a task. Sending a limousine out to pick him up is one possible action. Mailing him instructions for taking a bus is another.

A list of tasks for the Sunday school picnic:

Preparatory tasks

1. Have families sign up for food to bring
2. Arrange transportation for those needing rides
3. Purchase paper plates, etc.

Conduct tasks

1. Supervise in the kitchen when people show up with food

2. Organize a game time after supper

3. Clean up afterwards

PREPARATION PHASE

2. Scheduling preparatory tasks

What to write down: A task-completion schedule.

You need to take the list of tasks you prepared in the last stage and organize them chronologically so you can see what needs to be done when. For simpler events you can just use a calendar. For more complex events you may want to prepare a "sequence-of-tasks calendar" that uses a countdown approach.

Another part of scheduling tasks is assigning them to different people. You can write in their names on the calendar too.

A task-completion calendar for a Boy Scout outing:

MAY

SUN	MON	TUE	WED	THU	FRI	SAT
		1	2	3	4	5
7	8	9	10 Reserve campground	11	12	13
14	15	16	17	18	19	20
21	22 Pick up archery equipment	23	24	25	26 Buy food	27 Outing
28	29	30	31			

> **PREPARATION PHASE**

> 3. Taking pre-event actions

Now's the time to get down to work preparing for the event. If you've done your schedule properly, you should know what has to be done first. Get going on it, and try to stay on schedule.

> **PREPARATION PHASE**

> 4. Planning for contingencies

What to write down: Contingency plans.

Murphy's Law warns us that things are sure to go wrong. Think about some of the more likely things that could go wrong and develop plans for what to do if they do. Then you'll be ready when the time comes. And don't forget to assign someone as shot caller, the one who decides when it's time to use a contingency plan.

An example of a written contingency plan:

Contingency Plans
East Moose Falls Community Church Sunday School Picnic

Scenario	Contingency	Shot Caller
It rains before picnic starts or forecast is more than a 50% chance of rain	Postpone until rain date	Sunday school superintendent
It rains after picnic has begun	Move to West Moose Falls Bible Conference Grounds	"

Bus breaks down anytime before picnic and cannot be repaired	Rent bus from Kid Movers	"
Bus breaks down en route	Bus to be followed by station wagon carrying food, etc. Station wagon can transport drivers back to church to get cars to shuttle everyone to the park	Bus driver

---

CONDUCT PHASE

---

1. Executing the plan

If you've done the preparations right, you'll be ready when the day of the event arrives. Stick to the plan.

2. Supervising the event

If you're in charge, make sure that those working with you know what their jobs are and check to see if they've done the work.

3. Executing contingencies

When something goes wrong, roll out the contingency plan. If you don't have one, go through the steps of the decision-making model to reach a sound decision quickly and then implement it.

4. Taking post-event action

There's always work to do afterward: cleaning up, settling accounts, evaluating the event, submitting reports to the sponsoring body, sending mailings to participants. Whatever it is, don't forget to do it.